Getting it straight from the Bible

> I was neither a prophet nor a prophet's son, but I was a shepherd, and I also took care of sycamore-fig trees. But the Lord took me from tending the flock and said to me, 'Go, prophesy to my people Israel.' Now then, hear the word of the Lord... Amos 7;14, 15.

A. Colin Day

A. Colin Day 2020

www.colinday.co.uk

ISBN 978-1-5272-7019-0

Contents

	Foreword	1
1	What's special about the Bible?	3
2	How to interpret it	12
3	Christ and the Bible	22
4	The people of God	29
5	The promised land	38
6	Law and grace	47
7	Prosperity	59
8	Tithing	65
9	The Sabbath	73
10	The Bible and science	79
11	The last things	95
12	Miracles	102
13	The church	112
	Postscript	122

Foreword

The peace campaigner outside Purley post office assailed me with her rhetoric. When I told her I was a Christian she switched to a scriptural tack.

'Jesus said, "I came to bring peace" ', she informed me.

'He said, "I did *not* come to bring peace, but a sword" ', I replied.

'Oh, you can prove anything from the Bible!' was her retort.

Where does this idea come from, that you can 'prove anything from the Bible'? It is sadly true that those who hold the Bible to be the word of God can nevertheless come to very different conclusions on a number of matters. You don't have to remove 'not' from its words, as my peace campaigner did. The impression may be given that the scriptures are like modelling clay—you can mould them into whatever shape you want.

Does the Bible indicate that believers ought by right to receive great financial prosperity and material riches from God? Is it essential to give a tenth of your income to the local church if you are not to come under God's curse? Is all the evidence discovered by scientists to be dismissed if it goes against the literal words of the Bible? Bible-believing Christians have widely-differing views on these and many other subjects.

Now, I am not writing here about those who dismiss the claims of the Bible. I am writing about those who consider it to be the inspired word of God. Such differences of interpretation are a problem to Christians, who sense that something is amiss, yet do not know who (if anyone) is right. Worse than that, these matters bring the Bible into disrepute. If it is indeed God's message to man, then surely it should be clear and unambiguous.

The basic problem is how we should interpret the scriptures. Somehow, we have managed to get much of the message of the Bible into a tangle, and we need to get it straightened out. What is more, we have mixed the revelation from God with our traditions, accumulated over the years. We need to get the message straight from the Bible and not from other sources.

It is necessary here to give some indication of my background to show where I am coming from in writing these pages. I am not a professional theologian, but I have studied the Bible for many years. When assembling material for my book *Roget's Thesaurus of the Bible* I went through the Bible from cover to cover a number of times, investigating every verse, recording references and arranging them into topics. The result was compiling 115,224 Bible references (for comparison, the Bible has 31,102 verses) sorted into 11,000 topics. In doing this, I was not wanting to support any theological standpoint, but simply to put into categories what the Bible had to say. Going through every verse of the Bible several times, filing references under topic headings, assembling like with like, it would have been very hard to pursue particular theological positions. I was simply categorising what the Bible had to say on these topics. It is on the basis of this work that the present volume is being written. Let us see what happens if we lay aside what we have been accustomed to believing and see what the Bible and the Bible alone is saying about various matters.

This book simply examines a number of subjects. First of all, the basic matters of the inspiration of the Bible and its application to the Christian church are considered. These chapters should be read first, as they define basic principles for interpreting the scriptures. Several major themes are then made clear. Remaining chapters deal with a few areas which have proved to be problematic for Christians, showing the use of the principles and themes earlier outlined.

Unless otherwise indicated, quotations are from the NIV. However, just about any other translation of the Bible could have been used.

So I invite you to see with me how far we can get if we attempt to get things straight by assembling simply what the Bible says about them.

Scripture quotations in this publication are from the HOLY BIBLE, NEW INTERNATIONAL VERSION ® NIV ® Copyright © 1973, 1978, 1984 by International Bible Society ®. All rights reserved worldwide.

1

What's special about the Bible?

Several years ago a young man was attempting to beat the world record for riding on a Ferris wheel. He was provided with a telephone. After several days going round in circles, having beaten the record, he was asked if anyone had telephoned him. 'Only the nutters,' he replied.

If the Bible is merely a collection of ancient religious writings, then those who spend a great deal of time and effort studying it may well be classed as nutters. Such a study is only really worthwhile if it is true that the Bible is from God. The Bible itself in various places lays claim to be the inspired word of God.

'Inspiration'

What do we mean when we talk about the Bible being 'inspired'? We may talk about a musician giving an inspired performance, or a painter or sculptor producing an inspired work. What we usually mean in such cases is that the artist achieved a high level of skill and artistry.

This is not what we mean when we talk about the Bible being inspired. Though parts of it are wonderful poetry or memorable sayings, other parts are not. In some places the writers of the Bible even seem to have gone a bit wobbly with their grammar! Whatever skill the writers displayed, this is not what we mean by their 'inspiration'.

What we mean is that the Bible comprises God's message to us. Its words are the words of God. The scriptures (we believe) declare with truth and authority what is to be known about God. They declare to us what God wants us to know. They speak to us with the voice of God himself.

Why believe it to be inspired?

Why should anyone believe that the Bible is the inspired word of God? It is true that the Bible itself claims to be God's word, but we cannot depend on these claims alone. To do so would be circular reasoning. We would be saying, in effect, 'The Bible says it is the word of God, so what it says is true, and therefore it is correct when it says it is the word of God.' This gets us nowhere.

Other religions claim that their scriptures are inspired. Why should we believe the Bible rather than, say, the Koran or the Book of Mormon?

There are various reasons for considering some book to be special. It may be that it has been recommended to you by someone you respect highly—your parents, a beloved grandmother, a church leader you know well. Perhaps they have read the book daily and have found it a great help in their lives, so you decide to read it and follow what it says.

The trouble with this reason is that it is no better than second-hand. Isobel Kuhn was later to become a pioneer missionary to tribal groups in South-East Asia. When she first went to college, her modernist professor discovered that she believed the Bible. 'Oh, you just believe that because your papa and your mama told you so,' he told her. She realized that this was so, and for several years she backslid from her Christian faith. (*By Searching*, OMF, 1957)

Maybe you consider that the teachings which the scriptures contain are of a very high moral standard, second to none in all the philosophies of the world. You may think what a good world it would be if only everyone obeyed what you find in this book. So you decide to study it and follow its precepts.

The difficulty here is that it relies on you being a judge of morality. On further inspection, you may feel that some parts of the Bible are highly moral, but others do not come up to your standards. You may respect the teachings in the Sermon on the Mount, but feel less happy about what Leviticus and Romans have to say about homosexuality, for instance. How can you regard a book as God's authoritative word to mankind when it stands or falls by your opinion of it?

It could be that you have studied the ancient manuscripts in great depth and have come to see that they must be genuine and authentic. Not many of us have carried out such a study. Hardly any of us are equipped to do so. However, it may be that you have read of others who have spent their lives in such research and who have concluded that this book is unique. You trust their work, and decide that you also will take this book for your guide.

In the Alpha Course (Holy Trinity Brompton) evidence is presented to show that the manuscripts for the Bible give a much stronger foundation for the text than those for any other ancient work. This is a good and necessary exercise. However, this in itself cannot be a basis for taking the Bible as God's word (as the originators of the Alpha Course would, I am sure, be the first to admit). The manuscripts may be numerous, they may match each other well, they may describe contemporary events with historical accuracy—but this might also be true of other books. If you find good documentary evidence for the Trojan War, will you believe in the Greek gods? If you find that Caesar's *Gallic Wars* is well-attested, will you base your life on the Romans' religious practices?

If we are to accept the Bible as God's unique word, fit to live and die by, we need better reasons than these.

The best reason
The reasons mentioned above may be good enough for you to consider the Bible as better than any other book. They are valuable in helping you to consider the claims of inspiration, although they are not sufficient to show that it is inspired.

The point is that the Bible is not merely a book about God: it is intended to bring us into personal dealings with God. Those who have the best reason to consider that the Bible is the inspired word of God are those who have come into a relationship with him, and who know from first-hand experience that what the Bible says about God is true.

The Bible declares that you may come into a life-changing relationship with God through Jesus Christ. For example, Jesus prayed to the Father, 'This is eternal life, that they may know you, the only true God, and Jesus Christ, whom you have sent' (John 17:3). John tells us why he wrote his gospel: 'These are written that you may believe that Jesus is the Christ, the Son of God, and that by believing you may have life in his name.' (John 20:31) Perhaps you have done this. You have experienced his forgiveness and peace. Maybe you have known the fulness of the Holy Spirit and have tasted joy and delight, and a close intimacy with God. Then you read the Bible and find that what you have discovered in personal experience is written down there already. You find that the scripture gives you a perfectly reasonable explanation for what has been happening in your own life. What is more, you find that the promises given within this book can be relied on as trustworthy. You can depend on them, and find them working out in reality. You then come to see that the Spirit who is at work in your life must be the same Spirit who caused the Bible to be written.

Computer programmers faced with a new piece of computer technology usually start out by trying things out to see how it works. Some attempts are successful, but mysteries remain. It is at this stage that the programmer's proverb is called into play: 'When all else fails, read the manual.' The manual confirms that the successes which have been achieved are indeed what the software is intended to do. Further, it describes how other things might be accomplished. The programmer then tries these out and discovers that they work. In a similar way, the Bible confirms what we have found in our own experience, and indicates other things which are true and will work.

(In fact, it does this very much more plainly than many computer manuals do!)

Though the deciding factor for believing in the Bible needs to be personal experience, that does not mean that there is no place for objective evidence or thoughtful discernment. Reason alone will not bring you to Christ, but becoming a Christian does not mean you have to throw away your mind.

The view of Jesus

If we have come to know Jesus Christ as our Saviour and Lord, then as followers of him we will want to maintain the same attitude towards the Bible as he had. In fact, there are some who would say that our authority is Jesus rather than the Bible, as he is truly the Word of God. Either way, we need to find out what Jesus thought of the scriptures.

You may think that this is the circular reasoning mentioned above, finding out what the Bible says about the Bible. This is not the case. Jesus' words recorded in the New Testament are about the Bible which Jesus knew, which was the Old Testament.

Jesus is reported as saying that 'the Scripture cannot be broken' (John 10:35). Throughout the gospels he quotes the Old Testament as authoritative: 'It is written' (Matthew 4:4, 7, 10; 21:13; 26:31 etc.) Jesus as depicted in the New Testament undoubtedly referred to the Old Testament as if it were inspired.

Could this be simply because Jesus was a man of his own time? Was it because he grew up surrounded by those who believed in the inspiration of the Bible, and so he accepted its authority unthinkingly? Should we be expected to know better in this day and age?

Alternatively, could it be that Jesus adopted this position because throughout his earthly life he was speaking to those who accepted the authority of the Old Testament? Paul relates how he conformed to the situation of those around him so that he might win them (1 Corinthians 9:19–22), concluding, 'I have become all things to all men so that by all possible means I might save some.' Perhaps this was Jesus' motivation, which caused him not to question the Old Testament for the sake of those around him, rather than based on his own personal conviction?

The truth is that Jesus did not always conform to the views of those surrounding him. He taught the scriptures as one who had authority, and not as their scribes (Matthew 7:28–9). He did not confine himself to the bare word of the scriptures, as the Pharisees might, but ventured beyond it. For instance, he asserted that there were many widows in Israel in the days of Elijah (Luke 4:25) and many lepers in Israel in the time of Elisha (Luke 4:27), things which the Old Testament does not tell us. His treatment of the scriptures was amazingly radical.

Jesus' dealings with the Sadducees show more about his views. The Sadducees only accepted the first five books of the Old Testament (the Pentateuch), and denied the doctrine of the resurrection (Matthew 22:23; Mark 12:18; Luke 20:27). Jesus answers them from the Pentateuch (Exodus 3:6; Matthew 22:32; Mark 12:26; Luke 20:37). However, Jesus states that the reason why they are wrong is 'because you do not know the Scriptures or the power of God' (Mark 12:24). He then proceeds to give an exposition of Exodus 3:6 which by its discernment and radicalness leaves them astonished (Matthew 22:33). Are these the words of someone who only accepts the authority of the scriptures in order to conform to the views of those around him?

The Bible's claim

There are claims within the Bible that the Bible is inspired. This is not as circular as it sounds. These claims serve to bind the whole Bible together. It is hard to take one part as inspired and not another, if the one part you approve declares that another part is true. It is perhaps fair to say that it is easier to accept the inspiration of the whole of the Bible, or of none of the Bible, than it is to suppose that only one part is inspired.

Throughout Acts and the epistles the authors quote the Old Testament as authoritative. Paul affirms that all scripture is 'God-breathed' (2 Tim. 3:16). Peter seems to link Paul's letters with the Old Testament scriptures (2 Peter 3:16).

The 66 books comprising the Bible as we know it have historically been recognised as inspired by God by Christians through the ages. This is not just a matter of traditions held by the major churches. Those who come to put their trust in Christ as their personal Saviour have in the main acknowledged the canon of scripture as applying to these books and no others.

The nature of inspiration

If the Bible is indeed the inspired word of God, how did God inspire it? There is still something of the authors' personality and style evident in the manuscripts. This is apparent even in translation, as you can see by comparing the matter-of-fact style of Acts, for instance, with the very different style of John's first epistle (the kind of writing you might expect from a very old man). So the underlying message which God wants to get across is not affected by the individual style of the writer.

If the Bible were to be written for the first time nowadays, and the language used were to be English, you could imagine various books being produced by very different writers. One book might be written by someone from the south of England who was well-educated and who had had a classical education. Another could be written in Yorkshire dialect. A third could be written by an American. Apparently, this would be of little concern to God, who could speak his word no matter what style was used by the writer.

Just the very words?
Some would contend that the very words (and all the words) of the Bible are the only ones possible; the ones decreed and chosen by God.

Certainly, any view of true inspiration would need to include an assurance that God prevented the *wrong* words from being used. Wrong words would give the wrong message. But was every individual word selected by God? This idea leaves us with a number of problems.

It is hard to imagine that the original style of the writers could be preserved if the very words were decreed by God as the only ones to be used. In various thrillers (usually spy stories) the hero, captured by the villain, is forced to write a letter dictated to him. But when the letter is received by his friends, it can be seen that the style is not typical of the hero, and the document is therefore suspect. If the villain were very clever, he might try to dictate the letter in exactly the style which the hero would himself use. Is this what God is supposed to have done? Are we to suppose that when Acts was written God chose all the words, but made sure that when put together they were in the style of writing which Luke, the author, always used? Does this seem likely?

If we believe in verbal inspiration, then there is another problem we must face. If the original words of the Bible were all inspired, then we need to ask whether we still have all those words. For the most part, it seems that we do, but there are some exceptions. 1 Samuel 13:1 reads as follows: 'Saul was [thirty] years old when he became king, and he reigned over Israel for [forty-]two years.' A footnote indicates that the words in brackets are missing from the Hebrew.

No-one is likely to lose much sleep over the loss of the words in this verse. However, they do indicate that we do not quite have all the words which were once there. As a student, the basis of faith of the Christian Union which I joined was that we believed in the inspiration of the Bible 'as originally given.' Since we do not exactly have the Bible 'as originally given', this statement loses much of its value.

It has been said that the differences and omissions of the original manuscripts of the Bible make no difference to the doctrines. The problems are minimal, but they do serve as a caution if we are depending on the inspiration of the original words. Does it seem likely that God would choose the very words, yet not ensure that those very words would be available to us?

What about translation?
There is a much greater problem still for those who consider that the very words are all inspired. The inspired words would then be those used by the original writers, Hebrew in the Old Testament (with some passages in Aramaic), and Greek in the New Testament. How can these words be translated without losing the inspiration?

Words in one language almost never correspond exactly to words in another language. If they did, machine translation would be easy. An early attempt at translation by computer took an English sentence, translated it into Russian, and then translated it back again to see how the process was going. This caused the sentence 'The spirit is willing but the flesh is weak' to come back as 'The whisky is agreeable but the meat is bad.'

Sometimes the lack of equivalence between words means that a footnote may be needed in our translations. John 3:8 reads, 'The wind blows wherever it pleases. You hear the sound, but you cannot tell where it comes from or where it is going. So it is with everyone born of the Spirit.' This leaves us missing one fact which is apparent to anyone reading this verse in the original Greek. The word 'wind' and the word 'spirit' represent the same Greek word, *pneuma* (which has given us the word 'pneumatic').

If the words themselves are God's choice, and inspiration is vitally linked with this, then translation from one language to another is really impossible without losing the inspiration. (It has been said by some followers of Islam that the Koran cannot properly be translated, and should be read only in Arabic.)

The New Testament writers were quite willing to use a translation of the Old Testament. They wrote, of course, in Greek, and their quotations from the Old Testament were not usually from the Hebrew/Aramaic original, but from the Septuagint Version, a Greek translation. Jewish scholars in

Alexandria had produced this version. (Tradition said that there were 70 scholars, hence the name 'Septuagint' meaning 'seventy'.) The fact that the New Testament writers were happy to use this translation (which at times does not stick as closely as it might to the original language) shows that they were not excessively particular about the very words of the original.

Sometimes, it must be admitted, the actual words used *are* vitally important. An example is Galatians 3:16, quoting Genesis 12:7. Stress is laid here on the fact that the word 'seed' (in Hebrew or Greek) is singular, not plural. So one might say that not just the word but the very numeric aspect of the word is inspired. It is at such times when the actual wording is vital that translation becomes most difficult. This Galatians verse, for instance, causes the translators of the Revised Standard Version to use the word 'offsprings', which is hardly current English. The New International Version gives the rendering 'seed', which is true to the Greek, but which we do not use when referring to descendants. One cannot say that there is any one correct translation. Both renderings have something to be said for them.

At other times the writers do not seem overly concerned with the minutiae of wording. Paul, describing the events at the last supper, quotes Christ as saying, 'This cup is the new covenant in my blood' (1 Corinthians 11:25). Matthew and Mark give the wording as, 'This is my blood of the covenant' (Matthew 26:28; Mark 14:24; some manuscripts have 'new covenant'). Does it make any difference? No, because the meaning is the same.

Meaning more than words
This seems to me to lie at the centre of the nature of inspiration. God inspired the *meanings*, so that they should be right. Different authors have phrased these as they found best. Others may quote them using slightly different words. Translations may be made into other languages. The important thing is that the meaning should be conveyed intact, not necessarily that the very words should be preserved.

Meaning is sometimes conveyed by a single important word, but more often than not it is conveyed by a string of words. The sentence 'She certainly has it in for him' conveys a meaning of antagonism which is not carried by any individual word within it. One may change the words (using the same language or even another language) and not destroy the essential meaning. It is this meaning which I believe is more important than individual words. It is the meaning which (I believe) God inspired and preserved.

The inspiration of the Bible is, it seems to me, seen not merely in individual words or phrases, but in the overall sweep of the scriptures when they are interpreted in a sensible, self-consistent manner. This means that if we are to get the true benefit from the Bible we need to be able to interpret it in this kind of way. Easier said than done! How can you interpret the Bible aright? It is to this problem which we must now turn.

2

How to interpret it

Do we have any choice?
Hobson was a man who hired out horses in Cambridge. When someone came to hire a horse, the only one they could have was the one with which Hobson presented them—'Hobson's choice'. Henry Ford said, 'Any customer can have a car painted any colour that he wants so long as it is black.' Do we have any choice in interpreting the Bible, or is there only one way?

We certainly don't have the option of interpreting the Bible according to our personal whim. Peter tells us (2 Peter 1:20) that scripture prophecy is not a matter of one's own interpretation. The original writers of the scripture, the prophets, did not use their own interpretation of what was being revealed to them. At the present time we are not to interpret what we read in our own private, individual way. Neither the one who sends out the message nor the one who receives it are to put their own personal interpretation on the information.

Perhaps we have no choice at all in the way we interpret the scriptures. A Jehovah's Witness came to my door one day, and was fervent in quoting the scriptures to support her cause. When I suggested to her that right principles were needed for interpreting the Bible, she was dismissive. Her view was that the Bible interprets itself. It says what it says.

Of course, she was oblivious to the fact that she was interpreting the Bible her way, and could not consider anyone interpreting it any other way. You know what she meant, though, don't you? She meant that all the Bible should be interpreted *literally*.

Literal?
Unfortunately, the word 'literally' is one which has undergone a devaluation in recent years. It has been so overused that its meaning has been debased. In some circles it is now equivalent to 'very much'. 'I was literally walking on air,' someone may say. Or, feeling that this could do with even more emphasis, 'I was quite literally walking on air.' Such people have to be brought down to earth with a bump.

The term 'literal' is derived from 'letter'. You can see the connection when we talk about 'the letter of the law'. 'Literal' means 'according to the basic meaning of the letters and the words'. The word 'literally' may be paraphrased as 'physically' or 'in material fact'. The opposite to 'literal' is 'figurative', 'spiritual', 'metaphorical' or 'allegorical'.

We all know what a gate is like. It usually has hinges (unless it is a sliding gate), and it opens up. This is the literal meaning of the word 'gate'. However, when we speak of Gibraltar as the gate of the Mediterranean, we are using the word outside its basic meaning. Gibraltar neither has hinges nor does it slide. It does not open up. This is not literal, but is a metaphor. Does that mean that what we have said is untrue? No, not at all. There is literal truth and there is metaphorical truth.

The regular formula which is used when the media wish to pour scorn on evangelicals is to describe them as 'fundamentalist Christians who believe the Bible to be literally true.' Some Christians seem to think that the highest tribute one can give to the Bible is to interpret it all literally. To do so is to be the most evangelical of evangelicals, they reckon. This is certainly the easiest rule to follow when interpreting the Bible, but is it valid?

Should we take the whole of the Bible to be literally true? Let us try it and see where it leads us.

1. When it says that Jesus was walking on the water (John 6:19) it means that he was literally and physically walking on top of the water.
2. When Jesus said of the bread, 'This is my body' (Matthew 26:26), then this bread was literally and physically his body.
3. When God told the people of Israel that he had carried them on eagles' wings (Exodus 19:4), then he had literally and physically transported them on the wings of eagles.

What do you think of this method of interpretation? No doubt you were happy with number 1 (I hope you were!). You may have considerable reservations about number 2. What about number 3, though? Are such statements really to be taken literally?

There are undoubtedly times when the Bible must be interpreted literally. If you do not accept that Jesus did literally walk on water, then you make a nonsense of the rest of the passages which describe it. For instance, why did those in the boat worship him as the Son of God (Matthew 14:32)? But this does not mean that Biblical statements must always be taken literally.

Jesus corrected those who wrongly interpreted his words in a literal fashion. Some were offended at the idea of eating his flesh, because they took his words literally. To them he says, 'The Spirit gives life; the flesh counts for nothing. The words I have spoken to you are spirit and they are life' (John 6:63).

Some speak of interpretations in spiritual terms as 'spiritualising away' the words of the Bible. Jesus was not afraid to tell us when his words needed to be interpreted spiritually. Such treatment takes nothing away from the meaning, but rather can transform it into the most profitable form for us. The desire for literalness when the scriptures call out to be figuratively interpreted has perhaps caused even more harm than the desire to interpret figuratively those parts which need to be interpreted literally. The tragedy is that by being over-literal we may actually miss what God is saying to us through his word.

There is no doubt that the simplest rule for interpreting the Bible is 'Interpret it literally.' The only trouble is that this rule sometimes comes up with the wrong answer. It is impossible to interpret the whole of the Bible literally. The Bible itself cries out against such treatment. Simple the rule may be, but it gives the wrong results. As well may the drunk search for his house keys under the light, not because he dropped them there but because it was easier to see things there.

So the rule has now become, 'Interpret the Bible literally except for those times when you shouldn't.' Everyone can subscribe to this. The big problem is deciding when to interpret it literally and when not.

Work at it
Although we may not interpret the Bible in personal, oddball ways, we must personally seek how to arrive at that universal truth which God intends to convey. Paul himself exhorts Timothy to be 'a workman who does not need to be ashamed and who correctly handles the word of truth' (2 Timothy 2:15). So it is not always a simple task to understand the scriptures, and we need to work at it.

If personalized interpretation is out, we may pay attention to how other Christians have interpreted the scriptures. This does not mean that we must always follow the traditional interpretations held by major denominations. For one thing, church groupings often differ in their teachings, and it may be that they sometimes (perhaps unwittingly) interpret the scriptures so as to back up their own positions, rather than trying first and foremost to see what the scriptures say. Furthermore, some leaders in the denominations no longer give emphasis to the supreme authority of the Bible, so we can hardly trust their interpretations.

Should we always follow the interpretations advanced by other evangelicals? We should certainly consider what such people have proposed, but here again, they differ amongst themselves. The principle of always following where others have led is the principle used by sheep. Until recently it was believed lemmings acted like this on their excursions over cliff faces!

Whilst it is valuable to consider interpretations advanced by other believers and groups of believers, we cannot escape the fact that we need to evaluate these views for ourselves, using God's gifts of reason in dependence upon the Holy Spirit's enlightenment. So we are faced with a paradox. Personalized interpretation is out, but personal evaluation and discernment of interpretations is vital. This is similar to the state of affairs with regard to salvation. There is only one, universal, narrow gate which leads to life, but it is a personal responsibility for each one to enter in by it (Matthew 7:13–14).

Verses and themes

There are two separate but related matters to be considered here. We may be attempting to interpret particular verses (or passages), or we may be trying to discover what the Bible as a whole says about a particular theme (or topic or doctrine).

A theme depends on the interpretation of verses which are apparently on that theme. A verse is interpreted most reliably when the interpretation fits in with well-established Biblical themes.

This is not as circular as it sounds. Skyscrapers have historically been constructed on a framework of girders. It is vital that each girder is strong and so can play its part in the strength of the whole framework. On the other hand, the framework keeps each girder securely in place and gives it strength.

In the same way, Bible verses which have a clear interpretation can lend strength to the themes for which they form part. Clearly-defined themes can help us in being sure of the interpretation of isolated verses. Verses and themes are inter-related, and serve to confirm one another.

A secure foundation

The skyscrapers on Manhattan Island, New York, depend on the rock of the island for their stability. Though the buildings may rise scores of floors in the air, it is necessary to fix the foundations several floors into the rock. When building in London, which has clay where Manhattan has rock, it is necessary to bore very deeply to insert reinforced concrete piles.

Any suggested Bible theme depends for its strength on the key verses and passages which underpin it. Most of the strange ideas about what the Bible says have arisen because they are based on an insecure foundation.

For a strong foundation, we need to interpret what is hard to understand in the light of what is easy to understand, not the other way round. This gives us our first principle for interpretation:

1. Start with what is clear.

The clearest statements are for the most part in the New Testamen. See what the New Testament says about any theme, and interpret the Old Testament accordingly.

This approach has the advantage of learning from the experts. Christ and his apostles were the ones best fitted to know the nature of God's revelation. If we follow their interpretation of the scriptures, we cannot go far wrong.

This principle is surely not earth-shattering. It is only common-sense. When I am working on a jigsaw puzzle, I go for the easiest parts first. I will separate out the edge pieces, and fit them together. If there is a clearly-identifiable feature (a ship's hull, or a distinctively-coloured dress), I look for parts of these. Then other less easily identified parts may then be fitted into what has been constructed.

Imagine what it was like for the pilot of a plane before electronic aids came into being. He would look at the landscape below him for recognisable features. What was that small town down there? It could be one of several. Features that were clear beyond doubt were the key. A railway line, or a lake with a characteristic outline, could be his starting point. Once these were identified, less clear features would fall into place. Only one of those small towns would then fit the bill. Start with what is clear, and interpret less clear items so that they line up with the clear ones.

The Bible context
A second principle of interpretation could be:

2. Examine the context within the Bible.

It has been said 'A text without a context is a pretext'. When national leaders find some of their less fortunate assertions appearing in the media, their common defence is, 'Oh, but you are taking my words out of their context.' Bible verses can certainly be found to support whatever you like if you ignore their surroundings. The context which we should examine comprises several layers:

(a) Surrounding material

The clue to the right interpretation may be not far away, in nearby verses or chapters, or in the rest of the book. An example has been touched on already. In John 6:48-58 Jesus speaks of the need for people to eat his flesh and drink his blood. Not surprisingly, the Jews and even his own disciples had problems with this teaching. Is he advocating cannibalism? If we look a little further on in the chapter we find Jesus saying, 'The Spirit gives life; the flesh counts for nothing. The words I have spoken to you are spirit and they are life' (v. 63). The context shows that Jesus is speaking in spiritual terms, not in terms of literal flesh and blood.

(b) Other books

We may discern the right interpretation by comparing how the subject is treated in other books of the Bible. For example, are the kingdom of heaven and the kingdom of God different? If you compare corresponding passages in the gospels, you will find that Matthew uses 'the kingdom of heaven' where the other gospel writers use 'the kingdom of God', so there can be no difference between them. (Compare Matthew 13:11 with Luke 8:10, for example; but there are many other instances.)

(c) The whole Bible

The ultimate context is, of course, the whole Bible. If the Bible is indeed God's word, then we should expect it to give a unified message. The test of our interpretation of one passage is whether our ideas fit in with the whole flow of the scriptures. The test of any teaching supposed to come from the Bible is whether it matches what the whole of the Bible says.

What we are saying here is simply that our interpretation of single verses or passages should fit in with the themes which have been securely established.

The world context

The Bible cannot be considered on its own, insulated from all around it. God's word has come to us in our present world. As our third principle, we should:

3. Consider the context within the world around us.

Just as Jesus, the Son of God, came to us in physical form like other people, so the Bible, the word of God, makes use of the natural facilities in our world. In interpreting the Bible, we need to pay attention to:

(a) The words

A word in any language will seldom correspond exactly to a word in another language (such as *pneuma* in Greek corresponding to 'wind' or 'spirit' in English).

To interpret a passage, it is helpful if you know what the words in the original language are, and the variety of meanings these words may take. Even if you are not able to cope with such matters, it helps if you realise that few if any words have a fixed meaning.

Sometimes we may not be sure whether certain words were in the original, or whether they had to be inserted to make proper English sentences. It is as if we are making our way through the loft of a house. Whilst we tread on rafters, we are on safe ground, but if we tread on the plaster between, expect trouble!

The lesson is, beware of interpretations (or sermons!) which depend solely on particular words (unless you can be sure that these words are genuinely in the original). Not many of us can cope with Greek or Hebrew, but help is often at hand from the footnotes in our Bibles or from commentaries.

Some help may be gained from comparing different translations. The story is told of the lady whose favourite verse which had helped her through many trials was, 'And it came to pass . . .' Her reason was, 'It didn't come to stay!' If she had looked at other versions apart from the King James (Authorised) Version, she would not have found these words. The Hebrew simply means 'and it was . . .' or 'and then . . .'

(b) Idioms

'The English language is full of idiots,' a foreigner is supposed to have exclaimed. All languages have their idioms, i.e. sayings where the sum of meanings of the words does not correspond to the meaning of the whole ('She certainly has it in for him').

Hebrew has a common idiom, 'son of . . .' This means 'characterised by . . .' or 'partaking of the nature of . . .' For example, 'sons of worthlessness' (Judges 19:22) and 'sons of thunder' (Mark 3:17). 'Son of man' is used by God many times when addressing Ezekiel. It is also used by Jesus to refer to himself. The meaning is essentially 'human being', and when used by Jesus it implies his true humanity.

(c) The style of writing

One should consider whether the passage is intended as a historical record, in which case it would be normal to take its words as a literal description of events. Alternatively, it might be poetic, even cast in lines of poetry, in which case one should be prepared for instances of poetic licence, symbolism and allegory.

(d) The culture

Every nation has its own culture. Sometimes we may fail to understand parts of the Bible because we do not understand what the culture was like then.

For instance, there was the custom of taking off a sandal. This was done when someone did not fulfil their proper responsibilities, and was a means of shaming them. It is mentioned in Deuteronomy 25:5–10, and was carried out in Ruth 4:7–8.

Sometimes contemporary writings or archeological discoveries may help us bridge the gap. Commentaries will often give helpful information about cultural practices.

(e) The world

The same God who inspired the Bible is the God who made the universe, and who decreed the way it works. Scripture should not clash with the real world, and the real world should not clash with scripture. It is true that God can suspend natural laws to work miracles. But it is also true that the laws are God's laws, and generally these laws are not suspended. It is this fact which makes miracles different from ordinary daily life.

Some interpreters of the Bible give you the impression that they resent those who study the universe in order to discern the laws on which it is based. They seem to be constantly apprehensive lest any more be discovered, since they will only have to ridicule and deny it. Such people are generally motivated by a desire to interpret all the Bible literally, and as we have seen, such a standpoint is not feasible. However, the world is God's world as much as the Bible is God's word.

Psalm 19 is instructive in this regard. The first six verses speak of the universe. The skies declare the glory of God and proclaim the work of his hands. The following five verses speak of the scriptures and the way God uses his word to bring blessings to the heart. Both the physical world and the Bible are used by God to bring his revelation. They work in concert and not in contention.

If we interpret the Bible and the observable world in such a way as to make them contradict one another, then there must be something wrong with our interpretation. More will be said about this in a later chapter.

A broad foundation

What strikes you when you see a photo of the Eiffel tower in Paris? Your eye may be drawn to the height of the structure and its viewing platforms near the top. Look down at the bottom and you will see that for stability the tower spreads very wide.

Each verse needs a broad foundation when you interpret it. You need to consider it in the light of the contexts we have mentioned.

A theme needs to have a broad foundation. It should be supported by an adequate number of verses whose interpretation is clear. This gives us a fourth principle:

4. Examine how broad the foundation is.

It all comes down to the issue of evidence. How much evidence do you have for your interpretation, and how strong is the evidence? As in a court of law, lack of evidence may even count as contrary evidence. You could imagine Sherlock Holmes saying to Dr Watson, 'But why were there so few footprints?'

There is something which we may call 'The desert island test'. Suppose you are marooned on a desert island. You have never heard anything about the Bible before, yet on the island you find a copy of it, without any marginal notes or section headings. (Such incidents have ocasionally been reported.) Through reading the Bible alone, without preconceived ideas, would you inevitably come to see that a particular theme is plainly taught?

Does it matter?

There may be times when you have to admit that you do not know how to interpret a certain verse. Other people may seem to be quite certain, but somehow you cannot share their certainty. There are occasions when you should:

5. Be prepared to admit your ignorance.

For me, this is the case with a prophecy in Zechariah which appears to be about the end time. 'On that day [the Lord's] feet will stand on the Mount of

Olives, east of Jerusalem, and the Mount of Olives will be split in two from east to west, forming a great valley; with half of the mountain moving north and half moving south' (Zechariah 14:4).

Is this to be fulfilled literally or does it have a figurative meaning? I must confess that the matter is not clear to me. I can find few if any clear verses to which it can be related. Nothing seems to be said in the gospels or epistles about the Mount of Olives being split.

It does not seem to be of great importance how you interpret this verse. I know from passages which are much clearer that Christ will indeed return to earth in glory and power. The precise details of his appearance on earth remain unknown to me, but that does not change my responsibility to live for him here in the light of his future appearing. This leads to a further principle:

6. Judge how much it matters.

It is important that we assess the relevance of Bible material to our present living for the Lord. There are themes which are of vital importance. This is not to say that these minor matters should never be considered, but first things first.

From this point we will examine some basic truths which emerge from an application of these principles and which form a strong Biblical framework and lead to further principles of interpretation.

Summary of principles
In this chapter several principles for right interpretation have so far been proposed. For convenience, these are listed here.

1. *Start with what is clear.*
2. *Examine the context within the Bible.*
3. *Consider the context within the world around us.*
4. *Examine how broad the foundation is.*
5. *Be prepared to admit your ignorance.*
6. *Judge how much it matters.*

3

Christ and the Bible

The story is told of the time Calvin Coolidge, 30th President of the United States, returned from church. His wife greeted him with the question, 'What did the reverend preach about today?'

'Sin,' was the reply.

'Well, what did he say about sin?' returned his wife.

'He was against it.'

We can at least give the man credit for discerning the main theme, even if he was a little short on the details!

How good are you at following a trail? Peoples who live far from civilisation are often highly skilled at noticing tiny signs (broken twigs, footprints, disturbed undergrowth) and constructing the path which has been taken. This is a similar process to discerning a theme.

In the last chapter we talked about clearly interpreted verses or passages which lead us to trace a Bible theme. In this chapter we see a theme which is presented ready made and for which we are given just a few passages. It is up to us to learn from the nature of these clues and to fill in other evidence for the theme.

Christ throughout the Old Testament

After his resurrection Jesus found on the road to Emmaus some of his disciples who were deeply depressed and seemed to have quite lost the plot (Luke 24:13-27). He chides them with being 'slow of heart to believe all that the prophets have spoken' (v. 25). His summary of 'the prophets' is that the Christ had 'to suffer these things and then enter his glory' (v. 26). Then, beginning with 'Moses and all the Prophets' he explained to them what was said about him 'in all the Scriptures'.

How I would have loved to have been at that Bible study! Christ obviously saw himself as a dominant theme of the Old Testament. In particular he refers to his suffering, his death and his subsequent glorification.

When Christ later appears to all the disciples in the upper room he conducts a similar survey of the Old Testament. Luke 24:44–7 shows him speaking of 'everything . . . written about me in the Law of Moses, the Prophets and the Psalms.' He refers here to the three main divisions of the Hebrew Bible, the Law, the Prophets and the Writings (of which the book of Psalms is the largest part).

Jesus chided the Jews for studying the scriptures in the hope that in them they had eternal life, and missing the fact that 'These are the Scriptures that testify about me' (John 5:39). For Christ, to believe in the Old Testament scriptures was to believe in him: 'If you believed Moses, you would believe me, for he wrote about me' (John 5:46).

Others in the New Testament proclaimed the same truth. Philip's excited news to Nathanael was, 'We have found the one Moses wrote about in the Law, and about whom the prophets also wrote' (John 1:45). Paul 'tried to convince them about Jesus from the Law of Moses and the Prophets' (Acts 28:23).

There is no doubt that the Old Testament deals with many other matters apart from that of Christ. Nevertheless, it appears that this one theme goes through the whole just like the writing on a stick of seaside rock. (For American readers, British seaside rock is a long, thin cylinder of hard candy, with the name of the town in a different colour of candy running through the stick from one end to the other.)

Tantalisingly, though in the New Testament we are pointed to some verses and passages which are on this theme, we are left to fill in others ourselves. There must be many other such passages if the whole Old Testament does indeed point to Christ.

Now this is something which vitally affects us. Some Christians have reservations about the Old Testament. Perhaps some do not read it. However, the Old Testament is the only Bible which Christ and the early disciples had. Perhaps our problem has been that we have not been able to interpret it aright. If we have come into a relationship with God our Father through what his Son Jesus Christ has done for us, and if the Old Testament tells about the one to whom we owe supreme love and gratitude, then we ought to be digging these things out and relishing them. In the words of E. E. Hewitt,

More about Jesus in his Word,
Holding communion with my Lord,
Hearing his voice in every line,
Making each faithful saying mine.

John Bunyan in *The Holy War* gives his own quaint representation of this. He depicts the town of Mansoul welcoming Emmanuel, son of King Shaddai, into the town. Emmanuel entertains the inhabitants 'with some curious riddles of secrets'.

Emmanuel also expounded unto them some of those riddles himself; but, oh, how they were lightened; they could not have thought that such rarities could have been couched in so few and such ordinary words. I

told you before whom these riddles did concern; and as they were opened the people did evidently see it was so. Yea, they did gather that the things themselves were a kind of portraiture, and that of Emmanuel himself: for when they read in the scheme where the riddles were writ, and looked in the face of the Prince, things looked so like the one to the other, that Mansoul could not forbear but say—This is the Lamb, this is the Sacrifice, this is the Rock, this is the Red Cow, this is the Door, and this is the Way; with a great many other things more.

We may be assured that the theme of Christ appears throughout the Old Testament. It would be good to know which verses and passages in the Old Testament form part of this theme. This also we can learn from seeing how Christ and the writers of the New Testament refer to some passages, and then using their methods and viewpoint when examining other passages. We also need to discern what it is that is said about Christ in the Old Testament and how these matters are picked up in the New.

Who is this man?
From New Testament passages quoting the Old Testament we learn more about the nature of Christ. He is not simply a mere man.

Peter quotes Moses saying that, 'The Lord your God will raise up for you a prophet like me' (Acts 3:22, quoting Deuteronomy 18:15), and applies this to Jesus. Someone like Moses would certainly be an important personage, but more is to come.

Jesus accepted as his designation 'the Christ' (Matthew 16:16-17). 'Christ' in Greek, or 'Messiah' in Hebrew, means 'anointed one'. In the Old Testament those who were anointed with oil for service were prophets (e.g. 1 Kings 19:16), priests (e.g. 1 Chronicles 29:22) and kings (e.g. 1 Kings 1:34). The title of 'Christ' implied the one anointed by God and sent by God to deliver Israel.

The Christ is not only descended from David, but David himself addresses the Christ as 'Lord' (Matthew 22:43-4, quoting Psalm 110:1). Jesus declares himself as greater than Jonah (Matthew 12:41) and even greater than Solomon (Matthew 12:42). Moses may have been a servant in God's house, but Christ is Son over God's house (Hebrews 3:5-6).

A Jehovah's Witness friend of mine declared, 'There is no evidence in the Bible that Jesus is God.' Is there not? Even if you deny the clear statement in John 1:1 that 'the Word was God', there are plenty of other indications. The writer to the Hebrews declares that Psalm 45:6 ('Your throne, O God, will last for ever') is written about the Son, Jesus the Christ, who is addressed as none other than God. Thomas hailed him as 'My Lord and my God!' (John 20:28). Paul, describing how Christ humbled himself to take human form, describes him as 'Being in the form of God' (Eph. 2:5-6). Col. 1:15-17 says, 'He is the image of the invisible God'. Col. 2:9 tells us, 'In Christ all the fulness of the Deity lives in bodily form'.

Titus 2:13 speaks of 'The glorious appearing of our great God and Saviour, Jesus Christ'. Is this about the appearing of both God and Jesus? Nowhere else does the NT speak of the Second Coming being the appearing of God the Father. Moreover, the Greek construction for 'the God and Saviour' matches 'the God and Father' (e.g. in 1 Pet. 1:3), which is obviously not speaking of two different persons. In similar vein, 2 Pet. 1:1 speaks of 'The righteousness of our God and Saviour Jesus Christ'.

When John tried to worship angels, he was told, 'Do not do it . . . Worship God!' (Rev. 19:10; 22:9). The disciples, we are told, "Worshipped him, saying, 'Truly you are the Son of God' " (Matt. 14:32), without any rebuke from Christ. Every creature sings, 'To him who sits on the throne and to the Lamb be praise and honour and glory and power for ever and ever!' (Rev. 5:13), showing that the same worship due to God is due to the Lamb also.

One could go on producing much more evidence, but space here forbids it. When we examine the context of the whole of the Bible, especially the New Testament, we see that the deity of Christ is a powerful theme. How much does it matter? If Christ is not God and yet we have honoured him as God, then this is none other than blasphemy. We might, however, wonder why the Scriptures have not made it clearer that he is not in fact God, rather than giving us so many indications of his true deity.

If Christ is indeed God, and yet we have not honoured him as such, and have taught others that he is not God, then we have denied God the worship due to him.

This is a vital decision, and not one to be taken lightly. What do you make of Christ?

The sacrifice for sin

The New Testament is very clear that the Old Testament not only foretells the coming of Christ, but predicts his suffering, his death and resurrection. Christ was quite specific about what was written concerning him in the scriptures. 'This is what is written: The Christ will suffer and rise from the dead on the third day' (Luke 24:46-7).

Peter saw in the death of Christ 'how God fulfilled what he had foretold through all the prophets, saying that his Christ would suffer' (Acts 3:18). Peter described how the Spirit of Christ worked in the prophets, predicting 'the sufferings of Christ and the glories that would follow' (1 Peter 1:10-11). The core of the gospel is that 'Christ died for our sins according to the Scriptures' (1 Corinthians 15:3).

These references all describe the Old Testament message in general. Is it possible to be more specific, to pin down the very passages which the New Testament must have had in mind?

On the day of Pentecost Peter declared that David in Psalm 16:8-11 wrote about the resurrection of Christ. Philip found the Ethiopian eunuch reading Isaiah 53 (Acts 8:32-5), the chapter which deals with a 'man of sorrows' who bears our sins. 'Philip began with that very passage of Scripture and told him the good news of Jesus' (v. 35).

It is very clear throughout the New Testament that Christ's was a sacrificial death. He died for our sins. By his death he has atoned. We are ransomed and set free. What is there in the Old Testament to correspond to this?

The answer is simple: the animal sacrifices.

It appears to be this which John the Baptist had in mind when he saw Jesus coming towards him and said, 'Look, the Lamb of God, who takes away the sin of the world!' (John 1:29). Paul tells us that God sent 'his own Son in the likeness of sinful man to be a sin offering' (Romans 8:3). When the Israelites were about to leave Egypt the Passover lamb had to be killed. Now, Paul says, 'Christ, our Passover lamb, has been sacrificed' (1 Corinthians 5:7).

In the Old Testament much stress is laid on the blood of the sacrificial animal. 'The life of a creature is in the blood' (Leviticus 17:11). Blood shed meant life laid down, and in particular, life laid down on behalf of someone else. 'It is the blood that makes atonement for one's life' (Leviticus 17:11). The blood of Christ is similarly emphasised in the New Testament. Peter tells us we were redeemed 'with the precious blood of Christ, a lamb without blemish or defect' (1 Peter 1:19).

The writer to the Hebrews goes further. 'It is impossible for the blood of bulls and goats to take away sins,' he tells us (Hebrews 10:4). Instead, 'we have been made holy through the sacrifice of Jesus Christ' (Hebrews 10:10). In Chapter 9 he describes how the Jewish high priest would go into the holy of holies once a year on the Day of Atonement to offer blood to atone for sins (vv. 6-7). Now Christ, as our high priest, has offered his own blood to bring us into our inheritance (vv. 11-14).

In these passages and many more, the New Testament writers indicate that the sacrifices of the Old Testament were intended to point forward to Christ and his death on our behalf. This is a major theme running throughout the whole Bible.

A unique salvation
'All religions are much the same,' some would say. This is probably the politically correct thing to say. That way, you are being fair to all. Believe what you will, so they say, it makes no difference.

But why should it be considered that all religions are the same? All religions are about moral standards, they would say. This is to ignore the fact that the standards upheld by different religions can be poles apart, so that what one religion considers the highest kind of law is to another religion horrendous cruelty. Every religion shows man's search for God, some say. However, this is not completely true. Christianity is about God's search for man.

Let us lay our cards on the table straight away. Christianity, as revealed in the Bible, makes no pretence at being politically correct. Christ's way is a unique salvation. By 'salvation' is meant 'rescue', 'deliverance', 'a way to God'.

After all, if the message of the Bible is indeed true, and if Christ himself is God come down as man, paying for our sins by his own sacrificial death, then how could there be any alternative way of salvation? So Jesus declared, 'I am the way and the truth and the life. No-one comes to the Father except through me' (John 14:6). Peter insisted, 'Salvation is found in no-one else, for there is no other name under heaven given to men by which we must be saved' (Acts 4:12). The writer to the Hebrews asks, 'How shall we escape if we ignore such a great salvation?' (Hebrews 2:3).

Does this sound intolerant? Some aspects of truth cannot be other than intolerant. If we believe that two plus two equals four, and neither three nor five, then we must risk the charge of intolerance by saying so.

Once for all
You might think that in the Bible there are two ways of salvation. In the Old Testament there was the keeping of the Law, with its offerings of animal sacrifices. In the New, salvation is no longer by keeping the Law (as we shall see in a later chapter) but by trusting in Christ's sacrifice for us. How do these two fit together?

As we have seen, the animal sacrifices were a picture of the sacrifice of

Christ. In World War II those left behind would have a photo of their loved one, and would look at this regularly to remind them of the one far away. When their loved one came home after the war, the photo was no longer necessary.

The writer to the Hebrews makes it clear that the sacrifices under the Law were only a picture and never were effective. The sacrifices of the Old Testament could only provide a 'shadow' (Hebrews 10:1) of the reality, but Christ's sacrifice was that reality. A thirsty man cannot slake his thirst with any number of photographs of water; only the reality of water itself can suffice. 'It is impossible for the blood of bulls and goats to take away sins' (Hebrews 10:4).

The sacrifices needed to be made over and over again because they were ineffective. 'Day after day every priest stands and performs his religious duties; again and again he offers the same sacrifices, which can never take away sins' (Hebrews 10:11). Some jobs have to be repeated indefinitely. The painting of the cantilever railway bridge over the Firth of Forth near Edinburgh is one of these tasks. As soon as the painting from one side to the other has been completed, it must be started again. The sacrifices were a never-ending task also.

In contrast, Christ's sacrifice is described as 'once for all'. 'He has appeared once for all . . . to do away with sin by the sacrifice of himself' (Hebrew 9:26). 'When this priest had offered for all time one sacrifice for sins, he sat down at the right hand of God' (Hebrews 10:12). Sitting down here demonstrates that one's work is finished. (Compare the busy housewife who says, 'I haven't sat down all day!') The fact that Christ sat down at the right hand of God means that the work of atoning for sin is finished.

The conclusion is that in God's sight there cannot be any more sacrifices for sin. Christ has accomplished it all.

So what?

In this chapter we have seen that the theme of Christ runs through the whole of the Old Testament. All the sacrifices made point forward to his one supreme sacrifice for sin, once for all. This is a theme which will help us in interpreting other parts of the Bible. If we come across other ideas based on less secure evidence which contradict this theme, then we can be pretty sure that they are wrong.

4

The people of God

The subject of God's chosen people is a difficult one for many Christians. We know that God chose Israel to be his people long ago. How should we regard the nation of Israel nowadays? Does God still regard the Jews as his exclusively special people? Will he once again take up the Jews for his special dealings? Some Christians seem to regard this subject as so important that they spend a considerable amount of time and energy teaching and preaching about it, and following events in the Middle East with all-consuming interest.

This is another major theme which runs throughout the Bible. We need to follow the whole sweep of the subject, being careful to end up with the New Testament's position.

God's people in the Old Testament
The story of God's chosen people begins not with Israel but with Abraham. God called him from Ur, a town not far from Basrah in modern-day southern Iraq. When directing him to go to the land which is to be shown him, God promises: 'I will make you into a great nation . . . and all peoples on earth will be blessed through you' (Genesis 12:2–3). Note that this looks ahead to blessing not just for the nation which would result from Abraham, but for all nations.

Not all of Abraham's offspring experienced the fulfilment of this promise. Isaac was the chosen one, but Ishmael was excluded (Genesis 17:18–21). Jacob was chosen, but not Esau (Malachi 1:2–3). There is a pruning process at work.

Jacob was renamed Israel—'Prince with God' or 'He struggles with God'—when he wrestled with God (Genesis 32:28). The 12 sons of Israel became the 12 tribes of Israel. The whole nation was referred to by God as 'my people the Israelites' (Exodus 3:10).

The nation of Israel was intended to be God's own special people: 'If you obey me fully and keep my covenant, then out of all the nations you will be my treasured possession. Although the whole earth is mine, you will be for me a kingdom of priests and a holy nation' (Exodus 19:5–6). This destiny was not declared for all time unconditionally, but, as we see here, it was dependant on Israel obeying God's voice and keeping the covenant.

Every child born into Israel entered into the covenant; as a sign of this every boy was circumcised at the age of eight days (Genesis 17:10-14).

Downsizing

Suppose that in wartime a special mission is envisaged. Only a special kind of soldier will do to carry this out. So the commanding officer puts a body of troops through various tests, at each stage weeding out those who display inadequacies, until in the end he is left with a small group of those who fulfil his expectations. This is the theme of a number of stories and films (as exemplified by the tale of Gideon in Judges 7). God seems to have carried out a similar kind of process with his people.

Initially the people of God appear to be all the descendants of Abraham. But then the group undergoes a progressive trimming down. We have already seen the scope of the promise reduced as Isaac was selected, but not Ishmael; then Jacob, but not Esau. Then there were those who did not believe, but who died in the wilderness and never saw the promised land (Numbers 14:29–30).

A united kingdom existed not much longer than Solomon, since in the reign of his son Rehoboam the northern ten tribes (then termed 'Israel' or sometimes 'Ephraim') broke away from the southern two tribes of Judah and Benjamin (1 Kings 12:19). The northern kingdom went further and further away from the true worship of God, until they were eventually taken away into exile to the land of Assyria (2 Kings 17:6). There is no record of them ever returning from there. They are the 'lost' tribes of Israel.

The southern kingdom of Judah and Benjamin was known as 'Judah'. It is from this name that the remaining house of Israel is to this day known as the 'Jews'. Not all of Judah were faithful to the Lord. Isaiah speaks of only a remnant returning to God (Isaiah 10:20–2).

Hosea goes even further, and speaks of those who were formerly the people of God being his people no more: 'After she had weaned Lo-Ruhamah [Not loved], Gomer had another son. Then the Lord said, "Call him Lo-Ammi [Not my people], for you are not my people, and I am not your God." ' (Hosea 1:8–9).

Such statements show that belonging to God's people was not simply a matter of physical descent. People could be severed from God's people if they did not follow God. Paul sees the remnant in Elijah's time as similar to the remnant today—'chosen by grace' (Romans 11:2-6). The writer to the Hebrews records that those with whom God was angry in the wilderness in the time of Moses 'were not able to enter, because of their unbelief' (Hebrews 3:16-19). Being part of the family of Israel, physically descendants of Abraham, was not enough. They needed to show the family characteristics in their attitude towards God. Without this, they were no longer reckoned part of the people of God.

Christ as Israel

Have you ever thought of Christ as Israel? If the people of God are those who have a special relationship with him and who please him in what they are and what they do, then who better to fill this role than the Son of God himself? There are various passages of scripture which affirm that this is indeed what Christ is.

A figure appearing in various places in Isaiah is 'the servant of the Lord'. Sometimes this one is described as 'Israel, my servant' (Isaiah 41:8–9), as if the whole nation is being addressed. At other times, a single person appears in view: 'Here is my servant, whom I uphold, my chosen one in whom I delight; I will put my Spirit on him and he will bring justice to the nations. He will not shout or cry out or raise his voice in the streets. A bruised reed he will not break, and a smouldering wick he will not snuff out' (Isaiah 42:1–4).

These are the verses which Matthew sees fulfilled in Christ (Matthew 12:18–21). More is to follow. In Isaiah 52:13, we once more read, 'See, my servant'. The passage about this servant continues through the well-known chapter 53. This is the servant who was 'pierced for our transgressions . . . crushed for our iniquities' (v. 5).

That this passage is about Christ is beyond doubt. When Philip heard the Ethiopian eunuch reading this chapter he 'began with that very passage of Scripture and told him the good news about Jesus' (Acts 8:35).

One picture which the prophets use for Israel is that of a grape vine, as in Jeremiah 2:21. The parable in Isaiah 5:1–7 depicts Israel as a vineyard planted by the Lord of hosts, which should have produced the fruit of justice and righteousness. Israel as a whole failed to do this, as both Isaiah and Jeremiah declare. However, Jesus proclaims 'I am the true vine' (John 15:1), showing his claim to be all that Israel should have been.

Christ is regarded as representative of the whole people of God. The clearest passage to demonstrate this is: 'The promises were spoken to Abraham and to his seed. The Scripture does not say, "and to seeds", meaning many people, but "and to your seed", meaning one person, who is Christ' Galatians 3:16. This is rather daring of Paul, since the word 'seed' in Hebrew and Greek, as in English, does not need to be plural in order to refer to all offspring or issue. However, Paul is convinced that the promise in Genesis 12:7 is properly fulfilled in Christ as the seed of Abraham.

For all these reasons it is apparent that Christ is regarded in the Bible as the true Israel of God.

God's people in the New Testament

You don't have to read far in the New Testament to see that God now has a special people: the church. Most of the epistles were written to local churches. They are those 'loved by God' (Romans 1:7), 'the church of God' (1 Corinthians 1:2), 'the church . . . in God the Father and the Lord Jesus Christ' (1 Thessalonians 1:1).

It is only natural that the members of the church should be those who are Christians. So what is a Christian? Some consider that a Christian is someone who goes to church; but going to church does not make you a Christian any more than living in a garage makes you a motor-car. Some think that you become a Christian when you are baptised, but in the New Testament people were baptised when they believed (Mark 16:16; Acts 10:47; 16:33-4).

It was in Antioch that the term 'Christian' was first used. It was applied there (perhaps disparagingly) to those who were disciples of Christ (Acts 11:26). Christ's great commission was for his apostles to go out and make disciples of all nations (Matthew 28:19). A disciple is a student, a learner. Christians are those ready to learn of Christ.

Many other terms are used to describe Christians. Christians are believers, those who believe in Christ, those who receive him and become children of God: 'To all who received him, to those who believed in his name, he gave the right to become children of God' (John 1:12). Christians are those who are saved because they have believed: 'Believe in the Lord Jesus, and you will be saved' (Acts 16:31). These are those who 'call on the name of our Lord Jesus Christ' (1 Corinthians 1:2).

Christians are the elect, i.e. those chosen by God. Paul endured 'everything for the sake of the elect' (2 Timothy 2:10). The reason he was an apostle was 'for the faith of God's elect' (Titus 1:1). All Christians are called saints, as you will see by looking at every reference to the word 'saint' in the New Testament.

Israelites entered into the covenant at birth, which was confirmed when the boys were circumcised at eight days old. People become Christians by the new birth, being 'born again' (John 3:3). For believers in Christ, 'Neither circumcision nor uncircumcision means anything; what counts is a new creation' (Galatians 6:15).

The merging of the streams

It appears, then, that there are two groups of people who are properly described as the people of God. How do these relate to one another? There are various possibilities.

You might suppose that God, seeing the apostasy of Israel, rejected them once and for all, and replaced them with the church. Is this what has happened? Let Paul reply: 'Did God reject his people? By no means!' (Romans 11:1).

Some consider that this present age, the age of the church, is an interlude within the history of Israel. During this time, some would say, 'the prophetic clock has stopped ticking'. God's dealings with his people Israel are suspended, to be resumed when Christ comes again and takes the church to be with himself. Then, they say, God will once again take up his ancient people Israel. We will consider some of these matters more thoroughly in a later chapter. For the moment, suffice it to say that it is extremely hard to find any evidence from clear passages of scripture that this interpretation is true. On the contrary, we find very clear evidence about the relationship of Israel and the church.

The astonishing thing is that the New Testament reveals, not that Israel has been rejected, nor that Israel has been replaced by the church, but that Israel and the church have been fused together into a single whole. This new people of God, fashioned on Christ, is the culmination of God's purposes for his own special people.

Do you find this hard to believe? Then look at Ephesians 2:11-22. Paul speaks to Gentile (i.e. non-Jewish) Christians. When they were 'separate from Christ' (v.12), i.e. before they became Christians, they were 'excluded from citizenship in Israel and foreigners to the covenants of the promise' (v. 12). Now they have been 'brought near through the blood of Christ' (v. 13), they are 'no longer foreigners and aliens, but fellow-citizens with God's people' (v. 19). What can this mean but that they now possess citizenship in God's Israel? 'The Gentiles are heirs together with Israel, members together of one body, and sharers together in the promise in Christ Jesus' (Ephesians 3:6).

In chapters nine to eleven of Romans Paul expresses his concern for 'my brothers, those of my own race, the people of Israel' (9:3-4). These seem to be the chapters in Romans which are least read. Studies in the book often deal with chapters one to eight, and then resume at chapter twelve. The chapters in between, though not without difficult parts, give invaluable information about the relationship between Israel and the church.

In Romans 11:17-21 Paul uses the picture of an olive tree to represent God's people. Some branches have been 'broken off because of unbelief' (v. 19). The Gentile believers are like a 'wild olive shoot' (v. 17) which has been grafted in to the tree, and 'stand by faith' (v. 20). The lesson to be drawn here is that together Jews and Gentiles who believe comprise the whole of the people of God, in one line of descent from the Israel of the Old Testament. The church does not *replace* Israel: the church, comprising both Jews and Gentiles who believe, *is* now the true Israel of God.

Who are Jews?
The question which then arises is, what about those who are Jews, who are physically descended from Israel? The clear answer is that physical descent does not guarantee inclusion in God's people. Paul declares that 'Not all who are descended from Israel are Israel. Nor because they are his descendants are they all Abraham's children' (Romans 9:6-7). As we have seen, branches which by nature formed part of the olive tree may be broken off. This should not be surprising to us. After all, the same thing happened throughout the Old Testament.

The fact is that in the New Testament there are Jews and Jews. There are those who by physical descent count themselves as Jews, and there are those who are counted by God as part of his people because they follow the faith of the patriarchs. So Paul says, 'A man is not a Jew if he is only one outwardly' (Romans 2:28). Abraham is 'the father of all who believe but have not been circumcised' (Romans 4:11). 'Those who believe are children of Abraham' (Galatians 3:9). John the Baptist warned people not to trust in the fact that Abraham was their father, since 'out of these stones God can raise up children for Abraham' (Matthew 3:9). Jesus confronted people who said, 'Abraham is our father' (John 8:39) and told them, 'You belong to your father, the devil' (v. 44). Physical descent alone is far from being an adequate qualification for membership of God's people.

Then what about those descended from Israel? Are they now all excluded from God's people when all the promises were originally made to them? Paul faces this question at the start of Romans 11. 'Did God reject his people? By no means' (v. 1). He gives evidence for this conclusion: 'I am an Israelite myself . . . God did not reject his people, whom he foreknew' (v. 1). Those among the Jews who believe in Christ form part of the ancient people of God along with Gentiles who believe. Paul is himself an example of this. 'What Israel sought so earnestly it did not obtain, but the elect did. The rest were hardened' (v. 7).

The result is that many Jews rejected their Christ, but when the offer was thrown open to them, many Gentiles gladly received it. Have the Jews lost their opportunity for all time? 'Did they stumble so as to fall beyond recovery? Not at all!' (Romans 11:11). The Gentiles have taken advantage of the gospel: 'Because of their transgression, salvation has come to the Gentiles to make Israel envious' (v. 11). But the promise still remains of a great ingathering of Jews who will believe in Christ and re-enter into their ancient status as part of the church: 'If their transgression means riches for the world, and their loss means riches for the Gentiles, how much greater riches will their fulness bring!' (v. 12).

Paul had 'great sorrow and unceasing anguish' (Romans 9:2) because so many of his fellow-Jews had excluded themselves from the salvation God provided in Christ. They had every right to be part of God's kingdom (v.4), and even now the gospel is 'the power of God for salvation; first for the Jew, then for the Gentile' (Romans 1:16).

Paul concludes his illustration of the olive tree by explaining that at the moment a hardening has come upon many of the Jews. This will continue until 'the full number of the Gentiles come in. And so all Israel will be saved' (Romans 11:25–6). How are we to interpret the reference to 'all Israel' here? He has already made it clear that there is only one way to be saved—through Christ's salvation. You will find in Romans the clearest exposition of this truth in the whole of the Bible. Can we then suppose that God will change his mind and accept everyone on the basis of physical descent from Israel and the patriarchs? This interpretation falls foul of everything which has been said in Romans, and especially in chapters nine to eleven. It seems rather to refer to a great ingathering of Jews back into the true people of God which we have seen is now the church. Does it mean that every single physical descendant of Israel will believe in Christ? Such a claim would be extremely surprising. Many have already died in unbelief.

I suggest that what Paul is saying is that when the number of Gentile believers nears completion, then there will be a great ingathering of Jews into the church, and so the whole spiritual Israel of God will be complete—all the true Israel will be saved.

God's new people

Peter takes the words applied to Israel of the Old Testament: 'You will be my treasured possession . . . a kingdom of priests and a holy nation' (Exodus 19:5-6). He then uses these same concepts and applies them to the church: 'You are a chosen people, a royal priesthood, a holy nation, a people belonging to God' (1 Peter 2:9).

Jesus, speaking to the Jews, said: 'I have other sheep, that are not of this sheep pen. I must bring them also. They too will listen to my voice, and there shall be one flock and one shepherd' (John 10:16).

Jesus' purpose was 'for the scattered children of God, to bring them together and make them one' (John 11:52). Those Jews (the 'circumcised') and Gentiles (the 'uncircumcised') who share the faith of Abraham are brought together in a new manifestation of the people of God, still called 'Israel': 'Neither circumcision nor uncircumcision means anything, what counts is a new creation. Peace and mercy to all who follow this rule, even to the Israel of God' (Galatians 6:15–16)'.

The 'rule' or 'standard' which Paul speaks of here is that keeping the law is irrelevant (neither circumcision nor uncircumcision counting for anything), and that what is all-important is a 'new creation'. This term is used in 2 Corinthians 5:17, where Paul says that 'if anyone is in Christ, he is a new creation'. The Israel of God now consists of those, Jews and Gentiles alike, who have come to new birth by accepting Christ's salvation.

Revelation 7

In Revelation 7:3–8 we find 144,000 of the 'servants of our God' (v. 3) sealed on their foreheads, from 'all the tribes of Israel' (v. 4), 12,000 from each tribe. What are we to make of this multitude?

It is hard to take this passage as referring to literal descendants of Israel. For one thing, the tribe of Dan is omitted. Joseph is included as well as Manasseh, though the tribe of Joseph was for most purposes treated as the two tribes, Ephraim and Manasseh.

In Chapter 2 a warning was given to interpret what is unclear in the light of what is clear. The position regarding Israel is clear throughout the New Testament. A general picture emerges of the people of God as being those who are believers in Christ, and of God excluding those who are simply descended physically from Israel but do not have faith. Such a position is shown in the earlier chapters of Revelation, with references to 'those who say they are Jews and are not' (Revelation 2:9; 3:9). The church has a spiritual line of descent both from the 12 apostles and from the 12 tribes of Israel. This is shown in Revelation chapter 21, where the gates of the new Jerusalem are inscribed with the names of the 12 tribes of Israel (v. 12) and the foundations of the wall have the names of the 12 apostles of the Lamb (v. 14).

So I suggest that the 144,000 in Revelation 7 is to be taken figuratively as a picture of the church. The number itself may be taken to represent the completeness of the church, coupled with the fact that 12 is associated with the people of God. James also addresses his letter 'To the twelve tribes scattered among the nations' (James 1:1), though his message is obviously addressed to 'believers in our glorious Lord Jesus Christ' (James 2:1).

Does this interpretation strike you as credible? If not, can you suggest another interpretation which tallies with the rest of the New Testament?

Conclusion

There is now in God's sight 'no difference between Jew and Gentile' (Romans 10:12). Christ himself has 'made the two one and has destroyed the barrier, the dividing wall of hostility' (Ephesians 2:14).

I hope you will agree that there is ample evidence to conclude that there is now one people of God, comprising all, whether Jew or Gentile, who have believed in Christ and have come to God on the basis of his all-atoning sacrifice. Moreover, this new people of God is in true line of (spiritual) descent from Israel in the Old Testament. This fact is so clearly attested in the New Testament that we may use it as another of our pillars. Teaching which denies that there is only one people of God, the church, believers both Jew and Gentile, should be regarded as suspect.

5

The promised land

The thought of a promised land is one which has thrilled the hearts of men and women through the ages. The idea of Utopia, of a homeland, of Nirvana, a land where dreams come true, Shangri-La, paradise, heaven—who has not longed for such a place?

This was never more so than for the people of Israel. The promised land was to be the fulfilment of their dreams, a land flowing with milk and honey (Exodus 3:8 and many other places). From bondage and slavery in Egypt, they were to know peace and prosperity in the land called, at various times, Canaan, Israel and Palestine. Even today, when Jews have celebrated the Passover away from the land, their final greeting to one another is 'Next year in Jerusalem!'

In the Old Testament 'the land' is a central theme. This was the land of promise, given to Abraham and his descendants, lost at the exile, and regained at the return from exile. In particular, there are many prophecies concerning the return of Israel to the land. Some have seen the setting up of the nation of Israel in recent years, with immigrants returning to the land of Palestine, as a literal fulfilment of these prophecies. Is this a valid interpretation of the scriptures? Since so much emphasis is placed on this subject in the Bible, we might expect that it has relevance to us in this day and age, but how?

Once again we need to look at the subject in the light of the whole sweep of the Bible, making sure that we end up with the interpretation which is clearest in the New Testament.

The land provided

Abraham was told to leave his country and kin, and to 'go to the land I will show you' (Genesis 12:1). When he arrived, he was told, 'All the land that you see I will give to you and your offspring for ever' (Genesis 13:15). (This is the verse which Paul in Galatians 3:16 applies to Christ.)

Though Isaac and Jacob were sojourners (aliens and temporary residents) in the land, the people did not take possession of the land until the 'exodus'. When Israel had been several hundred years in virtual slavery in Egypt, God called Moses and told him, 'I have come down to rescue them from the hand of the Egyptians and to bring them up out of that land into a good and spacious land, a land flowing with milk and honey' (Exodus 3:8).

The word 'exodus' is from the Greek, and means 'departure'. Through the books of Exodus, Leviticus, Numbers, Deuteronomy and Joshua the message is of the exodus, departure from Egypt, preparation in the wilderness, and occupation of the promised land.

The exodus was a pivotal event in the history of Israel. God sent help to a people in bondage, displayed his power through the plagues on Egypt, divided the Red Sea for his people to escape, gave them the Law at Sinai, brought them into the land of promise and gave them victory over the people of the land.

This was the time when the children of Israel became not just a family but a nation—God's nation. So the themes of the people of God and the promised land are intertwined.

Each year the people had to celebrate the exodus from Egypt by keeping the Passover. Every household had to kill and eat the Passover lamb in memory of the time when the blood of the lamb was painted around the doorway so that God, when he destroyed the firstborn of the Egyptians, would 'pass over' the house protected by the blood (Exodus 12:1-13).

The significance of the land

Every nation considers its homeland as the most special country in the world. This is especially so for the Jews, as God gave them this territory. To this day one of the most notable daily newspapers in Israel has the name 'Ha'aretz' (Hebrew 'the land').

The people of Israel had a particular reason to consider their land to be marked out above all other lands. The land of Israel was to be a place different from all others because of God's presence. It is described as 'his holy land' (Psalm 78:54).

Within the land there was to be a place even more special. Whilst still in the wilderness the people were told of 'the place the Lord your God will choose from among all your tribes to put his Name there for his dwelling' (Deuteronomy 12:5). It was there that the sacrifices had to be offered (v. 6). This place was subsequently revealed as Jerusalem. 'I have chosen Jerusalem for my Name to be there' (2 Chronicles 6:6).

The importance of Jerusalem was that this was to be the place where the temple would be built, which God called 'a temple for my Name' (2 Chronicles 6:8). It was at the temple that the menfolk had to appear before God three times a year at the important feasts (Deuteronomy 16:16). It was on the altar in that temple that their burnt offerings had to be offered (Deuteronomy 12:26-7).

Holy as the temple was, there was one part of it which was called the 'holy of holies' or 'the Most Holy Place' (2 Chronicles 3:8). Into this, only the high priest was able to venture, and that only once a year (Hebrews 9:7) on the Day of Atonement (Leviticus 16:29–34), offering a sacrifice to make atonement for himself and for the people.

So the land may be viewed like an onion, with concentric layers. The land contained Jerusalem. Jerusalem contained the temple. The temple contained the holy of holies. Each successive layer is more holy, more set apart, more truly representing the place where God himself dwells. This good land, the land of promise, the land flowing with milk and honey, only acquires its most desirable attributes because it is the place in which God is to be found.

Losing the land

We saw in the previous chapter that God would not retain among his people those who turned against him. In the same way, possession of the land by Israel was always conditional. Though God had promised them the land 'for ever' (Genesis 13:15), there were strings attached. If they did not keep the law a penalty would ensue: 'You will be uprooted from the land you are entering to possess' (Deuteronomy 28:63). This is indeed what happened. The northern kingdom of ten tribes ('Israel' or 'Ephraim') was taken from the land to Assyria (2 Kings 17:6), with no record of them ever having returned. The southern kingdom ('Judah') lasted longer, but was eventually exiled to Babylon (1 Chronicles 9:1).

Return prophesied

Before they even entered the land the people were told that if exile ever took place, then if they returned to the Lord with all their heart the Lord would restore them to the land once again (Deuteronomy 30:1–5).

Before they suffered exile, there were prophecies of return to the land once more. Isaiah in particular has much to say on this theme. The return is couched in terms of a new exodus, like the old exodus from Egypt in some ways, yet in other ways outstandingly different. We will examine some of these themes later in this chapter.

The Land in the New Testament

We have seen how central is the theme of the land in the Old Testament. In interpreting the Bible we have said that it is vital to see how the New Testament rounds off such a theme. The promised land was rather like an onion with concentric layers. There was the land, the city, the temple and the holy of holies. Let us see how these various layers are taken up and interpreted in the New Testament.

(a) The land
The writer to the Hebrews considers all the 'heroes of faith' to be seeking a land. 'They admitted that they were aliens and strangers on earth' (Hebrews 11:13). 'They were longing for a better country—a heavenly one' (v. 16). The 'kingdom of God' for us is not to be an earthly kingdom, but the realm where God rules in human hearts. God has prepared for us a heavenly country.

In the last chapter it was shown that the New Testament reveals a merging of God's ancient people of Israel and new believers, forming the church, Jews and Gentiles who believe in Christ. If Israel has a continuing right to the earthly land of promise, then presumably the church should also have a claim on that land. Such an earthly fulfilment of the Old Testament promises is not supported by any clear passage in the New Testament. Rather, the people of God see what God has prepared for them spiritually. The new land they enjoy, a land flowing with milk and honey, is their salvation, purchased by Christ in his sacrifice on the cross. In the words of the song,
> *The Lord has given a land of good things,*
> *I will press in and make them mine.*

(b) Jerusalem
Jesus mourned over Jerusalem, 'You who kill the prophets and stone those sent to you' (Matthew 23:37). He longed to gather their children 'as a hen gathers her chicks under her wings' but they were not willing. His conclusion is, 'Look, your house is left to you desolate' (v. 38), no doubt a reference to the temple.

Jerusalem was a magnet for all Jews who wanted to worship God. Jesus told the woman of Samaria, 'A time is coming when you will worship the Father neither on this mountain nor in Jerusalem' (John 4:21). The kind of worshippers required by God are those who worship 'in spirit and in truth' (v. 23).

The New Testament sees a contrast between the literal geographical city of Jerusalem and its spiritual equivalent. The writer to the Hebrews tells those who believe in Christ: 'You have come to Mount Zion, to the heavenly Jerusalem, the city of the living God' (Hebrews 12:22).

Paul contrasts the Jews, in bondage to a literal Jerusalem, with a heavenly Jerusalem which brings us freedom: 'Hagar . . . corresponds to the present city of Jerusalem, because she is in slavery with her children. But the Jerusalem that is above is free, and she is our mother' (Galatians 4:25–6).

This is the city which John sees: 'I saw the Holy City, the new Jerusalem, coming down out of heaven from God . . . And I heard a loud voice from the throne saying, "Now the dwelling of God is with men, and he will live with them. They will be his people, and God himself will be with them and be their God" ' (Revelation 21:2–3).

Jerusalem is the place where God lives, and in the New Testament he lives with his people. This is not in the old, literal, physical city, but in the new Jerusalem, our spiritual abode.

(c) The temple

If the temple was the place where the animal sacrifices were to be offered, you might expect that such a place would not be needed after Christ offered once and for all a sacrifice for sin to end all sacrifices for sin.

The temple had another function, however. It was the place where God was to be found. What has the New Testament to say about this?

Jesus spoke of his body as a temple (John 2:19-21). He told the Jews, 'Destroy this temple, and I will raise it again in three days' (v. 19). Similarly, the believer's body is described as 'the temple of the Holy Spirit' (1 Corinthians 6:19).

In Ephesians 2:19-22 Paul speaks of the whole people of God built into 'a holy temple in the Lord' (v. 21), 'built on the foundation of the apostles and prophets, with Christ Jesus himself as the chief cornerstone' (v. 20). We are 'being built together to become a dwelling in which God lives by his Spirit' (v. 22).

As you might expect, the New Testament equivalent of the temple is not a literal one with stones and timber. After all, God 'does not live in temples built by hands' (Acts 17:24). God lives in his people. 'We are his house' (Hebrews 3:6).

(d) The holy of holies

If you have an exploded view of an engine it is no use whatsoever to drop oil on the drawing of the bearings as they appear on the diagram. What you have is simply a picture to show how the real thing functions.

The literal Most Holy Place within the temple is a picture of the place in heaven which Jesus entered to make atonement for us (Hebrews 9:12). It typifies the place closest to God. Now 'we have confidence to enter the Most Holy Place by the blood of Jesus' (Hebrews 10:19). This can hardly mean that, were a new temple to be built, we have a right to go into the holiest part of it. We would surely be lynched for blasphemy. This must have a spiritual significance. Because of Jesus' death for us, we are able with confidence to come right into God's presence.

It may seem that apart from this the New Testament has little to equate with the holy of holies in the temple. However, there is a clue in the shape of this room. It was a perfect cube: 'The inner sanctuary was twenty cubits long, twenty wide, and twenty high' (1 Kings 6:20).

The city of new Jerusalem is also described as being the same shape: 'He measured the city with the rod and found it to be 12,000 stadia in length, and as wide and high as it is long' (Revelation 21:16).

What value can we find in the idea of a city which is physically in the form of a cube, or perhaps a square pyramid with extremely steep sides? This seems of little help to us. On the other hand, there is deep meaning in the figurative interpretation: that God is as present throughout his new city, the new Jerusalem, as he was in the holy of holies in the temple.

Once again the pattern is for that which was literal and physical in the Old Testament to find its fulfilment in the New Testament in that which is no less real, but spiritual.

The new exodus
If you have ever thought that the Old Testament prophets make for dull reading, then you should try Isaiah from chapter 40 (though it really starts from chapter 35). Isaiah looks beyond the time of exile, when Judah is taken captive to the land of Assyria, to another exodus when the people will be brought back from Babylon across the desert to the land of Israel once more.

This new exodus is contrasted with the first exodus when 'God made a way though the sea' (Isaiah 43:16). But the people are told 'Forget the former things' (v. 18). 'See, I am doing a new thing! . . . I am making a way in the desert' (v. 19).

The new exodus would not involve trudging through a trackless waste of wilderness. There would be a highway, the 'Way of Holiness', on which the redeemed would walk as they returned to Jerusalem (Isaiah 35:8–10). More than that, the Lord himself would be in the midst of the returning exiles, carrying the young of his flock and gently leading those who are pregnant

(Isaiah 40:11). He would appear on the highway, so that watchmen on the ramparts of Jerusalem could send out the cry to the cities of Judah, 'Here is your God' (Isaiah 40:9).

The call goes out to start construction of this highway: 'A voice of one calling: "In the desert prepare the way for the Lord; make straight in the wilderness a highway for our God" ' (Isaiah 40:3).

You will not need me to tell you how this theme is taken up in the New Testament. All four gospel writers see this as fulfilled in John the Baptist (Matthew 3:3; Mark 1:3; Luke 3:4–6; John 1:23) who was the voice in the wilderness, preparing the way before Christ.

Notice the full implication of this. The gospel writers (and John the Baptist himself in John 1:23) are interpreting the passage in Isaiah 40 in a symbolic way. They are indicating that the highway through the wilderness could be given a figurative interpretation, and therefore the new exodus may be interpreted figuratively also.

In the wilderness of Sinai there were water shortages. The new exodus, though heading through a dry land, would be amply provided with water. 'Water will gush forth in the wilderness and streams in the desert' (Isaiah 35:6). 'The poor and needy search for water, but there is none; their tongues are parched with thirst. But I the Lord will answer them; I, the God of Israel, will not forsake them. I will make rivers flow on barren heights, and springs within the valleys' (Isaiah 41:17–18).

Should we interpret these verses only literally, or is there a figurative meaning behind the words? Interestingly enough, Isaiah himself gives us his figurative meaning: 'I will pour water on the thirsty land, and streams on the dry ground; I will pour out my Spirit upon your offspring, and my blessing on your descendants. They will spring up like grass in a meadow, like poplar trees by flowing streams' (Isaiah 44:3–4).

So Isaiah sees the water as a picture of the Spirit of God, and the lush vegetation as a picture of the people of God.

For a New Testament interpretation of this theme, let us take Jesus' words at the Feast of Tabernacles: ' "If a man is thirsty, let him come to me and drink. Whoever believes in me, as the Scripture has said, streams of living water will flow from within him." By this he meant the Spirit, whom those who believed in him were later to receive' (John 7:37–9). It is hard to pin down a specific scripture which Jesus is quoting here, but the subject of the Holy Spirit under the image of water is very similar to that in Isaiah.

Once again, an aspect of the new exodus is interpreted in a figurative way, and the implication is that the new exodus itself has a figurative significance. The new life and refreshment which water can bring in the wilderness is interpreted in New Testament terms as the satisfying of desires and the fulfilment of longings which the Holy Spirit brings.

As we saw in the previous chapter, these passages in Isaiah have much to say concerning 'the servant of the Lord'. The culmination is in chapter 53, where this servant is seen as the one 'pierced for our transgressions' (v. 5). These references are taken up in the New Testament, and we are left in no doubt that this suffering servant is none other than the Lord Jesus Christ.

The fact we must consider is as follows. Isaiah 53, perhaps the clearest prophecy within the Old Testament concerning Jesus and his atoning death for us, is contained within those chapters of Isaiah which deal with a new exodus and return of the people to the promised land. It appears that what is in focus here is not just a literal return to a particular geographical location, but people coming to God spiritually in a new manifestation of his redeeming power. On the mount of transfiguration Moses and Elijah appeared and spoke with Christ of 'his departure, which he was about to bring to fulfilment at Jerusalem' (Luke 9:31). To 'bring to fulfilment' a departure is somewhat surprising in itself, but the Greek word translated 'departure' here is none other than the word 'exodus'.

Just as in the Old Testament the exodus was initiated by the sacrifice of the Passover (Exodus 12:3–7), so now our new exodus is accomplished through the death of our Passover lamb, Christ (1 Corinthians 5:7).

So we may confidently say that the return to the promised land prophesied in the Old Testament is revealed as the people of God entering into all that Christ has provided for them by his death and resurrection.

Multiple interpretations?
One single prophecy may be fulfilled several times in different ways. Take, for example, Isaiah's prophecy about a young woman giving birth to a son (Isaiah 7:14). This was initially fulfilled in Isaiah's own day, so that before the boy grew to the age of discretion, the two kings invading Judah would be no threat any more (v. 16). Matthew then sees a further fulfilment of the same prophecy in the virgin birth of Jesus (Matthew 1:22-3).

This is also the case with the new exodus. Isaiah spoke of a return following the exile to Babylon. There was a return after 70 years. Ezra and Nehemiah record this exodus from Assyria back to the land of Israel. However, when you read the account of dribs and drabs of fearful people and their problems in and around Jerusalem, this certainly fell far short of the glorious return described by Isaiah.

Could it be, however, that the return of the Jews to the land of Israel in our day and age is another fulfilment of these prophecies? We need to consider the implications of such an idea.

The Bible indicates that God is over all nations of the earth and that he determines 'the times set for them and the exact places where they should live' (Acts 17:26). Those who see a fulfilment of scripture in the return of Jews to Palestine will not be satisfied by this general statement, however. They would link this return to the promised land with God dealing once again with Israel as a nation, and usually they have theories about what will happen to the Jews when the church is taken to be with the Lord.

It is hard to find much evidence at all to substantiate these theories from the New Testament. On the other hand, as we have seen in this chapter and the previous one, there is plenty of evidence to show that believing Jews and believing Gentiles are fused into one body which now constitutes the people of God. The promised land which is now given to God's people (Jew and Gentile) is a spiritual one.

Conclusions

We have attempted to find a method of interpreting the Bible which starts with what is clear, and considers the whole sweep of the scriptures, culminating in the New Testament view. This has led us to the conclusion that both Israel and the promised land are now to be interpreted spiritually rather than literally.

This is not in any way to downplay the truth of these themes. Quite the contrary! Rather than focusing on one family of people in one localised area, God declares his intention of adopting people from every race, tribe, kindred and tongue. The blessings he gives apply to every condition of life. If we fail to see that this is far more glorious than simply the return of one nation to one locality, then perhaps we have not yet entered much into what Christ has purchased for us.

The New Testament writers obviously saw a spiritual fulfilment of these things by the gospel. Our deliverance from the house of bondage has been accomplished by God's servant Jesus. We have been brought by him into our inheritance, our promised land. Whatever other interpretation there might be in addition, this would be insignificant in comparison. We insist that a figurative interpretation is valid because the New Testament declares this. Those who deny us this, deny us our birthright.

6

Law and grace

The school inspector had heard the teacher give a lesson on the Ten Commandments. He decided to test the class with a question himself. 'Who keeps the Ten Commandments?' he asked. One small boy put his hand up. 'Teacher does, in the cupboard,' was the answer.

Are rules and regulations a good thing? Petty restrictions imposed by bureaucracy (what we call 'red tape') do not seem a good thing. On the other hand, safety regulations can be vital. And 'the rule of law' is essential for democratic government.

The nation of Israel had a collection of laws which they were given by God himself. These are to be found in the first five books of the Bible (the Pentateuch). These laws were central to the life of the nation, and may be referred to collectively as the Law (with a capital 'L').

The nature of the Law

The part of the Law with which we are all most familiar is the ten commandments. These are listed in Exodus 20 and repeated in Deuteronomy 5. With commands such as 'you shall not murder; you shall not commit adultery; you shall not steal' these seem timeless in their relevance to all people.

The Law is much more than these ten commands, though. There are hundreds of other commandments of various kinds. There are regulations for the animal sacrifices, for the ministry of the priests in the tabernacle (and later, the temple) and for the regular feasts. There are instructions governing fair dealings between people. Various punishments are detailed for offences.

There are lists of clean and unclean animals, so that, for example, it is all right to eat venison (Deuteronomy 14:4-5) but not pork (v. 8). Instruction is given for those encamped in the wilderness as to how to relieve themselves (go to a designated place outside the camp, and use a shovel to cover it over—Deuteronomy 23:12-13).

The Law is very detailed, covering a great many situations. Knowing and understanding all these laws and their implications is a lifetime study. Being able to keep them all is a different matter entirely.

It was by the Law that Israel learned God's standards. More than that, Israel learned that the Lord is a God of justice, that he cares about how people live, and that he has a heart for the downtrodden and the poor. The

Law also contained much which looked ahead to God's future provision of grace.

Central to the Law are the two concepts of blessing and curse. Those who kept the Law would be blessed. Those who did not would be cursed. When the Israelites came into the land the blessing and the curse were publicly read out on Mount Gerizim and Mount Ebal (Joshua 8:33–5). These were the blessings and curses which Moses had declared in Deuteronomy chapter 27 (for the curses) and chapter 28 (for the blessings). Being under the Law was a very serious business indeed.

The unity of the Law

If you are arrested on a charge of speeding, it is no use pleading in your defence that you have not murdered anyone. You are charged under the law which you have broken, and the fact that you have kept other laws is quite irrelevant.

When we come to the Law revealed in the Bible, the situation is even sterner. Despite the diversity of laws, 'the Law' is a unitary whole. If you are going to fulfil the requirements of the Law, you cannot pick and choose. It is all or nothing. 'I declare to every man who lets himself be circumcised that he is obligated to obey the whole law' (Galatians 5:3). The opposite side of this coin is shown in James 2:10: 'Whoever keeps the whole law and yet stumbles at just one point is guilty of breaking all of it.'

If out of all the hundreds of commandments there is just one which you do not keep, you will be charged not just with breaking this one, but with breaking the Law as a whole.

What use is a balloon with one part of its surface missing? What can you expect if you cut a piece out of a soap bubble? How can a clock function if you remove one cog wheel from the middle of the train? In just such a way, the Law is a whole in which every part is vital.

The covenant of law

A covenant is an agreement between two parties, each side promising to play his part. The duties to be performed by one party might be very different from those of the other party, but each side agrees to do what has been promised.

God made a covenant with the people of Israel at Mount Sinai after they had come out of Egypt. This covenant was based on the Law which was given then. In fact the Ten Commandments are described as 'the words of the covenant' (Exodus 34:28). Israel's part in the covenant was to keep the Law, and the Ten Commandments served as a summary of that Law.

In Leviticus 26 we have a fuller description of the covenant and the responsibilities to which each side was a party. Blessings would come from God 'if you follow my decrees and are careful to obey my commands' (v. 3). In particular, God promises, 'I will walk among you and be your God, and you will be my people' (v. 12).

Under the old covenant, life was promised to those who kept the Law. 'Keep my decrees and laws, for the man who obeys them will live by them' (Leviticus 18:5).

Some laws were of particular importance. Keeping the Sabbath was a sign of the covenant between God and his people at Mount Sinai (Exodus 31:13–17). Circumcision was a sign of the covenant between God and Abraham (Genesis 17:11), but also became part of the law (Leviticus 12:3).

Christ emphasises the Law

At times Jesus emphasised the Law and its strictness. He recognised the Law as being given by God and affirmed it: 'Do not think that I have come to abolish the Law or the Prophets; I have not come to abolish them but to fulfil them. I tell you the truth, until heaven and earth disappear, not the smallest letter, not the least stroke of a pen, will by any means disappear from the law until everything is accomplished' (Matthew 5:17–18).

In the Sermon on the Mount (Matthew chapters 5, 6 and 7) Christ pointed out that mere external observance of the Law was not enough. God requires the intention to be right also. It is not enough to avoid murder: anger and insult must be avoided also (Matthew 5:21–2). It is not enough to avoid adultery: lustful looks are equivalent to adultery (Matthew 5:27–8).

When a man asked Jesus what he should do to get eternal life (Matthew 19:16), Jesus' reply was, 'If you want to enter life, obey the commandments' (v. 17), and particularly mentioned some of the ten commandments (vv. 18-19). However, Jesus' final word was the necessity to dispose of his riches and follow him (v. 21).

One day an expert in the Law asked Christ which was the greatest of the commandments (Matthew 22:35-6). His reply was, 'Love the Lord your God with all your heart' (v. 37). The second most important commandment was 'Love your neighbour as yourself' (v. 39).

Christ himself added a new commandment for his followers: 'A new commandment I give you: Love one another. As I have loved you, so you must love one another' (John 13:34).

Christ's attitude was that the Law showed the moral nature of God and his intentions for his people. However, those who intended to observe the commandments needed to do so wholeheartedly and with complete thoroughness.

Christ annuls the Law
Christ indicated that the era of the Law was coming to an end. His attitude towards the Sabbath was regarded as unorthodox. In the view of the Jews he was 'breaking the Sabbath' (John 5:18), both by healing on that day (John 5:9 and many other references) and by not stopping his disciples from doing on that day what the Jews regarded as work (Mark 2:23–4). He declared that 'the Sabbath was made for man, not man for the Sabbath' (Mark 2:27), and announced that he, the Son of man, was 'Lord even of the Sabbath' (Mark 2:28).

Part of the Law was a poll tax (Exodus 30:12–15). Everyone had to pay half a shekel (or its equivalent, two drachmas). The rich were not to give more, nor the poor less (v. 15). Christ's disciples encountered those collecting this tax (Matthew 17:24–7). Peter, when questioned, was sure that his teacher would pay the tax (vv. 24-5). Later, in private, Jesus asked Peter, 'From whom do the kings of the earth collect duty and taxes—from their own sons or from others?' (v. 25). 'From others,' Peter replies. 'Then,' says Jesus, 'the sons are exempt' (v. 26). In order not to give offence to the tax-collectors, Christ has Peter pay the tax, but the implication remains. Those who are children of the King are free from the Law.

Clearer still is Christ's attitude towards the food laws. In response to the Pharisees who performed elaborate cleansing, Christ tells the crowd that nothing physically entering a person can make him (ceremonially) unclean (Mark 7:14–19). Mark adds, lest we fail to see the significance of these words, 'In saying this, Jesus declared all foods "clean" ' (v. 19). This the Law certainly did not do.

So Christ considered the Law as showing what the heart should be like before God, rather than a requirement that all its commands be obeyed literally. Moreover, he shows that he considers the legal requirements (concerning food at least) to be abrogated from now on. As we have seen, the Law is a unitary whole. If those parts of the Law concerning food and the half-shekel tax are no longer in effect, how can any part of the Law still be operative?

Christ's effect on the Law

In the Old Testament, God's people were obliged to keep the Law as their part of the covenant entered into at Sinai. The New Testament declares that Christ brought to an end this state of affairs.

The Law brought a curse on all those who did not keep it. Now Christ has bought our freedom from any such curse: 'Christ redeemed us from the curse of the law by becoming a curse for us, for it is written: "Cursed is everyone who is hanged on a tree" ' (Galatians 3:13).

Paul pictures the Law's demands on us being nailed to the cross, and thereby annulled: 'God made you alive with Christ. He forgave us all our sins, having cancelled the written code, with its regulations, that was against us and that stood opposed to us; he took it away, nailing it to the cross' (Colossians 2:13–14).

'Christ is the end of the law' (Romans 10:4). The word 'end' (Greek *telos*) may have either of two senses, and both are fitting here. On the one hand, the 'goal' at which the Law aimed, a life of complete righteousness, was fulfilled in Christ. Besides this, Christ is the 'termination' of the Law for us. Christ's way of making Jew and Gentile one is by 'abolishing in his flesh the law with its commandments and regulations' (Ephesians 2:15).

Grace

Now we come on to something which seems too good to be true. It is so unusual that some fail to understand it. It is so unexpectedly good that some, when they understand it, refuse to believe it. Yet it is undeniably what the Bible teaches.

Since Christ died and rose again, God does not deal with his people on the basis of the Law. He deals with them according to grace. What is grace? It is kindness you don't deserve, unmerited favour. 'The law was given through Moses,' says the apostle John. 'Grace and truth came through Jesus Christ' (John 1:17).

That we are undeserving is made abundantly clear. We have broken God's laws; we are sinners. There is only one way we can be saved, and that is by God's intervention on our behalf. 'All have sinned and fall short of the glory of God, and are justified freely by his grace through the redemption that came by Christ Jesus' (Romans 3:23-4).

Throughout the epistles the message is plain. We had sinned, and deserved to die. Christ died in our place, taking the punishment which was our due. Paul describes it as follows: 'You know the grace of our Lord Jesus Christ, that though he was rich, yet for your sakes he became poor, so that you through his poverty might become rich' (2 Corinthians 8:9). Christ came to fulfil the Law (Matthew 5:17), and he has fulfilled it on our behalf.

Some have used the letters G-R-A-C-E to spell out what the word means: *G*od's *R*iches *A*t *C*hrist's *E*xpense.

Is it fair? If you mean by fair 'an adequate return for services rendered', then of course it isn't fair. According to this definition of fairness, punishment for wrongdoings would be fair; forgiveness and mercy are not fair.

Is it unjust? By no means. Sin has not been overlooked, but has been punished. God has shown himself to be both 'just and the one who justifies those who have faith in Jesus' (Romans 3:26).

An illustration of this has appeared in very many sermons. A judge had a son who left home and gave himself up to a life of dissipation. He fell foul of the law. When he appeared in court, it happened that his own father was the judge. His father heard the case thoroughly, pronounced his son guilty, and ordered him to pay the largest fine allowable for the offence. Then the judge declared the case closed, came down into the floor of the court, took out his cheque book and himself paid the fine.

Saved by grace

In our day and age, despite all the offers of 'free gifts' (what other kind of gift is there?) which are part of advertising, we are assured that 'you get what you pay for' and 'there is no such thing as a free lunch.' We are immersed in a culture of paying for goods and for work done.

This was very much the situation with regard to God's laws. 'The man who obeys them will live by them' (Leviticus 18:5). Salvation in those days (being part of God's people and looked after by him) was supplied to those who paid the fee—obeying the Law.

This is an arrangement which has so been drummed-in to us that we find it extremely hard to accept a salvation which is not on the basis of payment for work done. However, in the New Testament there is great emphasis on salvation by grace, not by obeying the Law. 'It is by grace you have been saved, through faith' (Ephesians 2:8) Paul declares. 'And this not from yourselves, it is the gift of God—not by works, so that no-one can boast' (vv. 8-9).

'He saved us, not because of righteous things we had done, but because of his mercy' (Titus 3:5). We are 'justified by faith apart from observing the law' (Romans 3:28). God's grace and mercy is the reason for our salvation. Our faith is simply the straw by which we drink it in.

(Some knowledgeable reader may be saying here, 'But what about James?' Patience, friend; the matter will be dealt with later in this chapter.)

Christ, by his death on our behalf, has paid all there was to pay to secure your forgiveness and new life. What could your good deeds add to what he has done? If, by grace and favour, you were invited to a state banquet, would you consider leaving a tip for the Queen? That would be insulting. It is equally insulting to think that your good works can fill up any inadequacy in Christ's sacrifice.

What use is the Law?

If God no longer saves his people through them keeping the Law, what is the value of the Law to us today?

The Law revealed in no uncertain way what God is like. He is the God with high moral standards, who hates stealing, murder and adultery. He is the One who alone is to be worshipped, and who offers cleansing from sin by the offering of a perfect substitute as a sacrifice. He is concerned about personal relationships, even between those at enmity with one another. Above all, he is the God of justice.

Paul reveals that the Law was God's instrument in causing him to realise that he was a sinner (Romans 7:7-13). He would not have thought of coveting were it not that the Law said 'Do not covet' (v. 7). When you tell a child specifically not to do something, you can be sure that that is the very thing which they want to do. So it was with Paul regarding coveting.

We could not become righteous by observing the Law, but the Law could show us our sinful nature and how much we needed to be saved. 'Through the law we become conscious of sin' (Romans 3:20). So 'the law was put in charge to lead us to Christ that we might be justified by faith' (Galatians 3:24).

Not under the Law

It is plain that we cannot earn our salvation by keeping the Law. However, if the Law shows God's character, as Christians should we not be bound by the Law? Should not we who are made righteous through the atoning death of Christ show our gratitude to God by keeping the Law?

It is very difficult to shake off the idea that we still are subject to the Law in some respects. Some have suggested that the ceremonial law no longer applies to us, but the moral law does. The problem here is, how do you decide which laws are moral and which ceremonial? No such distinction is made in the scriptures.

Some would say that it is the ten commandments which are binding on us. These are, however, only part of the Law. There are other commandments which have a relevance to us today such as not showing favouritism in a lawsuit (Exodus 23:3). How do we decide which part of the Law is binding on us and which not?

Others have suggested that we have to keep that part of the Law which Christ did not fulfil. We are free of the laws which Christ fulfilled for us, they say, but the other laws still apply. Once again, we have the difficulty of knowing which laws are which. There is a law against boiling a young goat in its mother's milk (Exodus 23:19; 34:26; Deuteronomy 14:21). Did Christ fulfil this law or did he not? Are we obliged to keep this law because Christ did not fulfil it? We are into the realm of the ludicrous.

These attitudes neglect the fact that the Law is a unitary whole. The Law which Christ fulfilled was the *whole* Law. But ought we still to keep that Law?

This matter came to a head in the early church when some, notably Paul and Barnabas, preached the good news of Christ to Gentiles. The opinion of some Jewish believers who belonged to the party of the Pharisees was that 'the Gentiles must be circumcised and required to obey the law of Moses' (Acts 15:5). The apostles and elders in Jerusalem gathered to discuss this problem (v. 6) in what has been called the Council of Jerusalem.

Peter's reaction to this matter was that requiring the Gentiles to keep the Law was 'putting upon the necks of the disciples a yoke that neither we nor our fathers have been able to bear' (v. 10). So even for the Jews the Law had become an intolerable burden. The decision of the council was that Gentile believers did not need to keep the Law of Moses.

The council did instruct Gentile believers 'to abstain from food sacrificed to idols, from blood, from the meat of strangled animals and from sexual immorality' (v. 29). Were they being told to keep part of the law? This hardly seems conceivable, since the law is a unity and the council had certainly decided that Gentile believers were not to be given the burden of keeping it. It seems rather that it was being pointed out that they should avoid conduct which would particularly offend Jews, many of whom then shared the faith with them. 'All food is clean, but it is wrong for a man to eat anything that causes someone else to stumble' (Romans 14:20).

The Galatian Christians had been paying attention to some people (the 'circumcision party') who insisted that believers should keep the Law, and in particular, should be circumcised. You may see little harm, when people have already been saved through faith in Christ, in requiring them keep one or two little parts of the Law. What does it matter? Paul saw it quite differently. He considered that the circumcision party were preaching 'a different gospel' (Galatians 1:6), that they wanted 'to pervert the gospel of Christ' (v. 7), and as for every one who taught such things, 'let him be eternally condemned!' (v. 9). A requirement to keep part of the Law is a requirement to keep all of it: 'I declare to every man who lets himself be circumcised that he is obligated to obey the whole law' (Galatians 5:3). In fact, such a turning back to the Law implies a turning away from Christ (Galatians 5:2-4).

Any requirement that we *must* keep part of the Law, no matter how small a part, implies that our salvation through Christ is inadequate. It is not acceptable to say, 'Christ has purchased all your salvation for you, so it is available free to you—except that you *must* fulfil this part of the Law.' This is very important to keep in mind when we consider some of the subjects in the next few chapters.

Law in the heart

One of the most wicked characters in history was the Russian monk, Rasputin. Yet he preached the doctrine of the grace of God. His idea was that when he sinned, then repented and was forgiven, he received more of the grace of God. So, according to Rasputin, the more sin, the more grace.

Paul faces this suggestion in Romans 6.'What then? Shall we sin because we are not under law but under grace?' he asks (v. 15). His conclusion is decisive: 'By no means!'

God is a God of justice, who commands, 'Follow justice and justice alone' (Deuteronomy 16:20). We have seen that the Law gives an indication of his standards. Yet we are not tied down to the Law any more. How is God to achieve righteousness in our lives?

When a person believes in Christ, 'his faith is credited as righteousness' (Romans 4:5). We exchange our sin for Christ's righteousness through his sacrificial death on our behalf. 'God made him who had no sin to be [a sin offering] for us, so that we might become the righteousness of God' (2 Corinthians 5:21). If God went to such lengths to put righteousness to our spiritual bank account, would he not also see to it that we were able to live out righteousness in our daily lives?

One of the clearest indications of how God accomplishes this is to be found in Jeremiah 31:31-4 (quoted in Hebrews 8:8-12). Here God declares that he will make 'a new covenant with the house of Israel' (v. 31). This will not be like the old covenant based on the written Law, which Israel had broken (v. 32). This time God says, 'I will put my law in their minds and write it on their hearts' (v. 33).

Rather than imposing external demands on people to keep the Law, God is going to use a different strategy altogether. He is going to work from the inside. He is going to change the hearts of people so that they will do what is right. This he will do by causing the Holy Spirit to be resident within them. 'I will put my Spirit in you and move you to follow my decrees' (Ezek. 36:27).

One should not suppose from these Old Testament references that God intends all his regulations to be so imprinted on the hearts of his people that their obedience will be a literal one, keeping every last rule to the letter. Rather, their hearts will be changed so that they will want to do the will of God: 'It is God who works in you to will and to act according to his good purpose' (Philippians 2:13). It is because of this that James refers to 'the law that gives freedom' (James 1:25; 2:12).

God's purpose throughout has been: 'That the righteous requirements of the law might be fully met in us, who do not live according to the sinful nature but according to the Spirit' (Romans 8:4). In particular, God produces this in our hearts by means of love. 'God has poured out his love into our hearts by the Holy Spirit' (Romans 5:5). Christ's summary of the Law was wholehearted love for God and our neighbour (Matthew 22:35-6). This is echoed by Paul: 'He who loves his fellow man has fulfilled the law' (Romans 13:8–10).

We who belong to Christ, who have his Spirit within our hearts, are the only ones who have the power to live so as to please God: 'Sin shall not be your master, because you are not under law but under grace' (Romans 6:14). This is the argument in Romans chapters 6 to 8. Through Christ we have died to sin and been set free. We have died to the Law and have been raised so as to bring forth fruit for God. We are not now to live according to the flesh but according to the Spirit. His Spirit will give life to our mortal bodies and cause us to live for him.

God did not intend the good news of freedom from the Law to develop into an excuse for licentiousness. Far from it! 'Do not use your freedom to indulge the sinful nature' (Galatians 5:13). 'Live as free men, but do not use your freedom as a cover-up for evil' (1 Peter 2:16).

And James?

Paul declares, 'We maintain that a man is justified by faith' (Romans 3:28). James, on the other hand, declares, 'You see that a person is justified by what he does' (James 2:24). Martin Luther, eager to assert justification by faith, called James' letter 'an epistle of straw', or, to choose a fruitier translation of Luther's words, 'a right strawy epistle'.

How can we reconcile these two statements which seemingly are poles apart? We decided in Chapter 2 that we need to start with what is clear. Both statements are clear enough, though seemingly contradictory. However, Paul goes into great detail and has considerable arguments to show that the Law is not the way to be justified (declared righteous) before God. So could it be that we have not investigated James' statements in sufficient depth?

The passage in question is James 2:14-26. What James is questioning is the value of claiming to have faith when this is not backed up with deeds (v. 14). What we *think* James is doing is contrasting faith and works. If you look more closely at the passage you will see that James is contrasting faith unaccompanied by deeds with faith demonstrated by deeds. 'Faith by itself, if it is not accompanied by action, is dead' (v. 17). 'Faith without deeds is useless' (v. 20).

True faith should be accompanied by deeds. James is not speaking of deeds without faith. He says, 'I will show you my faith by what I do' (v. 18). In this way, Abraham was shown to be righteous by what he did 'and not by faith alone' (v. 24). 'His faith was made complete by what he did' (v. 22).

We are declared righteous (justified) in God's eyes when we believe in Christ. We are declared righteous in men's eyes when our faith results in actions. We are saved by faith alone, but true faith never will rest alone. How can it be seen that God has forgiven us and made us new creatures in Christ unless his Spirit living in our hearts makes a change in our lives?

So Paul and James can shake hands. They are not teaching contradictory doctrines, but only emphasising the two sides of the one truth.

Conclusions

The Law was given in the Old Testament to demonstrate God's standards and to show his requirements of holiness for his people. However, the Law is no longer the way God deals with his people, the church. We are not under any obligation to fulfil the Law, but rather we need to receive God's grace toward us and to live in the light and power of that grace.

This is a point very forcefully made in the New Testament. To return in any way to living under the Law is a denial of God's grace. To consider that God lays the law down for his children is to turn our backs on his kindness and love in Christ.

We are in no way to consider that God's kindness is an excuse for conduct which displeases him. Our lives are to be beyond reproach. But this is to be accomplished not by a slavish adherence to rules and regulations, but by means of God's Spirit empowering us to live for Christ.

Lessons so far
In these last four chapters we have been investigating major themes which run through the Bible. We have been trying to get things straight from the Bible, seeking to deal honestly with what the Bible presents. As we have done so, differences between the Old and New Testaments have become apparent.

The Testaments are interlinked, but their approaches are very different. One provides a commentary on the other. As an old rhyme puts it:
The New is in the Old concealed;
The Old is in the New revealed.

There is a phase change between the Old and New Testaments. A phase change is seen when ice melts to become water. Both substances are chemically the same, but their physical properties are radically different. The New Testament very commonly focuses on what is spiritual rather than on what is literal. Often, matters which are shown literally in the Old Testament (the temple, sacrifices for sin etc.) are seen to be spiritually understood in the New.

We need to bear this phase change in mind when considering other themes. As Christians we need to make sure that our interpretations lie comfortably alongside the New Testament.

The major themes which have been hammered out in these four chapters are like great girders forming part of the skeleton of a skyscraper. Interpretations of other themes should be locked securely into these if they are to be secure. The themes we have found are:
    a Christ is the ***major theme*** of all the scriptures.
    b Christ offered ***one sacrifice*** for sin, once for all.
    c There is ***one way of salvation*** through Christ.
    d There is ***one people of God***, the church of Christ, Jew and Gentile.
    e We are now ***not under the Law, but under grace***.

7

Prosperity

'Money is the root of all evil'—so proclaimed the popular song. A bit of a travesty really, because what the King James version said was, 'The love of money is the root of all evil' (1 Timothy 6:10). George Bernard Shaw is said to have declared, 'Lack of money is the root of all evil'.

It is because people love money so much that pyramid schemes or chain letters flourish. You know the way these things work. You receive a letter requesting you to send money to someone several steps further up the pyramid, and to broaden the base of the pyramid by copying the letter and sending it to a number of other people. Then, in due time, you expect to receive from those further down the pyramid several times the money you paid out. Many people are taken in by this idea, not stopping to think that there must be a limit to the number of those who receive several times what they give. (Those who hope to win large sums on the lottery also do not seem to consider that the money to enrich them only comes from the large number of people who lose their stake.)

A common idea which seems to be increasingly popular in some circles is that God shows his favour to us by increasing our material riches. So the bigger, the more expensive, the flashier car which the minister drives, the more God must be blessing his ministry. This is the so-called 'prosperity teaching', represented by its opponents as 'name-it-claim-it-get-rich-quick'. How far does this concept agree with what the Bible teaches?

We have suggested (in Chapter 2) several principles which we should follow when trying to interpret the Bible. We have traced (in chapters 3 to 6) five major themes which are basic to the Bible's message. From this chapter on we will seek to apply these ground rules to a number of issues which will serve as suitable examples for demonstrating how the principles for interpretation are to be applied. More importantly, these issues have been chosen because they have caused and are causing problems for Christians, often generating much pain and distress. Prosperity teaching is the first of these.

Prosperity in the Old Testament

There are many places in the Old Testament where we find the promise of material prosperity for those who are righteous, that is, those who keep God's Law. One notable example is in the blessing which was to take place on Mount Gerizim. 'If you fully obey the Lord your God and carefully follow all his commands,' they were told (Deuteronomy 28:1), then 'the

Lord will grant you abundant prosperity—in the fruit of your womb, the young of your livestock, and the crops of your ground—in the land he swore to your forefathers to give you' (v. 11). Certainly in the Old Testament wealth could be a sign of God's blessing.

Poverty would be an unknown thing: 'There should be no poor among you ... if only you fully obey the Lord your God and are careful to follow all these commands I am giving you today' (Deuteronomy 15:4–5).

Before you get carried away with this, remember that the blessings promised on Mount Gerizim were offset by the curses declared on Mount Ebal. Note that all such prosperity is promised to those who keep the Law. It is of the nature of the Law that there are both blessings and curses. We are not now under the Law, and so we are not subject either to its blessings or curses. We need to hold our fire until we see what the New Testament has to say about this matter.

Some have seen in the prayer of Jabez an encouragement to seek prosperity: 'Jabez cried out to the God of Israel, "Oh that you would bless me and enlarge my territory! Let your hand be with me, and keep me from harm so that I will be free from pain." And God granted his request' (1 Chronicles 4:10).

This is, however, just a single verse. Remember we need to look at how much evidence there is for any theme. Once again, we need to see how the New Testament regards this subject.

Undoubtedly the Old Testament is given to us for our profit. But should we expect this to be profit which lines our pockets?

Warnings about riches

The disciples of Jesus were well aware of the Old Testament link between God's blessing and material prosperity. When the rich young man went away sorrowful, not being able to respond to Christ's claims, Christ astonished his disciples (Mark 10:23–7). He told them, 'It is easier for a camel to go through the eye of a needle than for a rich man to enter the kingdom of God' (v. 25). In their amazement they asked, 'Who then can be saved?' (v. 26). If the one who has been so blessed by God that he has abundant riches can hardly be saved, then who can?

The trouble with riches is that one may easily rely on them. Paul has to instruct Timothy, 'Command those who are rich in this present world not to be arrogant nor to put their hope in wealth, which is so uncertain, but to put their hope in God, who richly provides us with everything for our enjoyment' (1 Timothy 6:17).

Jesus taught that the seed sown among thorns is choked by 'the worries of this life, the deceitfulness of wealth and the desire for other things' (Mark 4:19). So riches are certainly not the unmitigated blessing which some see them to be. Individuals who have won the lottery may often serve as examples of this. Riches beyond the dreams of avarice do not necessarily free people from problems in this life.

James in his epistle is extremely strong in his remarks to the rich. He charges them with having 'hoarded wealth in the last days' (James 5:3). In other words, these are the last days, near to the time when Christ will come again. We should be about his business, on tiptoe with expectation. This is no time to be merely busying ourselves by amassing wealth. Such a concern is tantamount to getting 'involved in civilian affairs' when a Christian's aim should be 'to please his commanding officer' (2 Timothy 2:4). James' condemnation is, 'You have lived on earth in luxury and self-indulgence' (James 5:5).

If possession of riches can be dangerous to one's spiritual health, seeking riches is no less a risk. 'People who want to get rich fall into temptation and a trap and into many foolish and harmful desires that plunge men into ruin and destruction. For the love of money is a root of all kinds of evil. Some people, eager for money, have wandered from the faith and pierced themselves with many griefs'(1 Timothy 6:9–10).

In view of these verses it is hard to imagine Christ or his apostles urging us to seek material prosperity as a sign of God's blessing on us. If riches are a danger to the soul, can we expect a loving heavenly Father to reward us in such a way? Even a desire to be rich can ruin our spiritual lives.

Examples

If material prosperity is a sign of God's favour, then we might expect that Christ would be the supreme example of this. However, the reverse is the case. He was born in a stable. His baby clothes were only strips of cloth. These matters were to be the very evidence that he was a Saviour, Christ the Lord (Luke 2:12). When he was in the flow of his adult ministry, he did not even have a half shekel ('two-drachma') for the tax (Matthew 17:24–7). He certainly did not have a denarius, but had to ask for one to be brought in order to use it as a visual aid (Mark 12:15). He cautioned a would-be follower that he had nowhere to lay his head (Matthew 8:20), the implication being that his followers could not be certain of this either.

'You know the grace of our Lord Jesus Christ', Paul says, 'that though he was rich, yet for your sakes he became poor, so that you through his poverty might become rich' (2 Corinthians 8:9). Are we to interpret this verse literally? Although Christ was poor in this world's goods, maybe it was in order that we might attain material riches?

This was certainly not Paul's experience. He explains to those who had sent him financial help, 'I know what it is to be in need, and I know what it is to have plenty' (Philippians 4:12). The experience of apostles is that 'we go hungry and thirsty, we are in rags' (1 Corinthians 4:11). In fact, Paul says, 'We commend ourselves . . . in hunger' (2 Corinthians 6:4-5). Does it really seem that God wishes to commend his servants by a display of wealth?

God's provision
Though the New Testament does not promise that we will be materially wealthy, it makes it abundantly clear that God will provide for his servants. 1 Timothy 6:17, already quoted, reminds us that God 'richly provides us with everything for our enjoyment'. Those who give to others will find an ample supply for themselves: 'God is able to make all grace abound to you, so that in all things at all times, having all that you need, you will abound in every good work' (2 Corinthians 9:8).

In words which could be particularly relevant to the prosperity movement, Paul warns Timothy about those who imagine 'that godliness is a means to financial gain' (1 Timothy 6:5). Before the verses quoted above on the danger of desiring to be rich, he says: 'Godliness with contentment is great gain. For we brought nothing into the world, and we can take nothing out of it. But if we have food and clothing, we will be content with that' (1 Timothy 6:6–8).

Being content with the basic provision for life, and with the presence of the one who can provide for us, is a theme echoed by the writer to the Hebrews: 'Keep your lives free from the love of money and be content with what you have, because God has said, "Never will I leave you; never will I forsake you" ' (Hebrews 13:5).

After the rich young man had gone sorrowfully away, and Jesus had told his disciples how hard it was for a rich man to enter the kingdom, the disciples wondered how they would fare in terms of material provision. Jesus told them that anyone who had left home or family or property for his sake would receive 'a hundred times as much in this present age (homes, brothers, sisters, mothers, children and fields)' (Mark 10:30).

A hundred times more material benefits than one has given up for the gospel—that sounds like riches! However, one must bear in mind that Jesus has just that moment told them of the difficulty rich people would have entering the kingdom of God. Would he choose that same time to promise them that they would become rich?

I suggest that Jesus was reminding them that God is no man's debtor. They had followed Jesus in a way which the young rich man found impossible, by leaving everything. Jesus is saying that throughout this life, though there will be persecutions ahead, there will be ample provision for their material needs, and with a loving family of God's people to make up for the family left behind.

True riches

Christ contrasted 'worldly wealth' with 'true riches' (Luke 16:11). He contrasted treasure on earth with treasure in heaven: 'Do not store up for yourselves treasures on earth, where moth and rust destroy, and where thieves break in and steal. But store up for yourselves treasures in heaven... For where your treasure is, there your heart will be also' (Matthew 6:19–21).

The church in Smyrna is told: 'I know your afflictions and your poverty—yet you are rich!' (Revelation 2:9). On the other hand, the church in Laodicea is told: 'You say, "I am rich; I have acquired wealth and do not need a thing." But you do not realise that you are wretched, pitiful, poor, blind and naked' (Revelation 3:17).

So it seems that there are two kinds of wealth. You may be a millionaire in one kind, yet be a pauper in the other. There are real spiritual riches, riches in heaven, which are of far more value and much longer lasting than earthly wealth. God has 'chosen those who are poor in the eyes of the world to be rich in faith,' James tell us (James 2:5). The parable of the rich fool (Luke 12:13–21) ends with the death and impoverishment of the man, and with the statement: 'This is how it will be with anyone who stores up things for himself but is not rich towards God' (v. 21).

So there are riches which are much more than this world's wealth, and which are far more to be sought after. This is surely the way we are enriched in Christ: 'Though he was rich, yet for your sakes he became poor, so that you through his poverty might become rich' (2 Corinthians 8:9).

It is far more important for a believer in Christ to seek for these spiritual riches rather than looking for material wealth. 'In him you have been enriched in every way,' says Paul to the Corinthians (1 Corinthians 1:5).

God may also commit earthly wealth to us, in which case we have a responsibility to act as faithful stewards. However, 'Though your riches increase, do not set your heart on them' (Psalm 62:10). Our heart should be where our treasure us. Our true riches are Christ himself, the real treasure in heaven. Where is your heart?

Conclusions

We have seen again that the material provision of the Old Testament is matched by spiritual provision in the New. By nature we have hearts that long for material riches. God is in the process of showing us that what we have in Christ is so much more than these things. In particular, he promises to provide for us day by day as he lives with us, and as he dwells in us by the Holy Spirit.

And finally ...

Suppose you have a church where the minister is convinced about prosperity teaching. He preaches that the more you give to God, the more you will get. His congregation give until it hurts. The minister gets the flashy car which (he reckons) shows that God is blessing his ministry. His congregation are left with a hole in their bank balances, waiting for someone to give to them. Doesn't this sound rather similar to a pyramid scheme? Have you thought of that?

8

Tithing

The Law specified both a poll tax and income tax. The poll tax was the requirement for everyone to give neither more nor less than half a shekel. Chapter 6 showed how Christ gave indication that this was not to apply to God's children any more.

Income tax was at the rate of 10%. Tithing is giving one tenth (a tithe) of your income or property. It is especially used to describe giving a tenth to God. There are some churches, especially some of the new ones, which teach that it is required of all Christians, rich and poor, to give 10% of their income to the local church. Unless this is done, they say, you lack commitment to Christ and God will not bless you.

You can probably see some of the problem areas which need to be examined. Tithing is part of the law, and we saw in Chapter 6 that we are no longer under the law. Keeping part of the law carries with it the need to keep all the law, because the law is a unitary whole.

In this chapter we shall examine the extent to which tithing is a theme which goes through the whole Bible, and whether it is binding on believers in Christ. The case for tithing is made very clearly in the book *The Gift of Giving* (formerly called *Tithing*) by R. T. Kendall (Hodder & Stoughton 1998). I have used that book to sample the arguments advanced by those who pursue such teaching. The assertions regarding tithing which are listed below are drawn from that book.

Tithing in the Old Testament
There are in fact not many places where tithing appears in the Old Testament, so we may easily review them all. The first mention of the subject is when Abraham gave a tenth of everything to Melchizedek, priest of God Most High (Gen. 14:18–20). Then when Jacob had his dream at Bethel he vowed that of all God gave him he would give a tenth back (Genesis 28:20–2).

Within the Law, one tenth of all produce was to be given to the Lord (Leviticus 27:30–3). This tithe was to be given to the Levites in return for their service (Numbers 18:21, 24). From this Levites were to give a tenth, the 'tithe of the tithe', to the Lord, to be presented to Aaron the priest (Numbers 18:26–8).

In Deuteronomy 12:5–19 (and again in 14:22–7) the tithe is represented as a fund from which a meal was to be enjoyed before God. The Levite was to be invited to join the family of the one presenting the tithe. Deuteronomy

14:28 (and again in 26:12) describes a further practice to be followed every three years whereby the Levite, the sojourner, the fatherless and the widow may be provided for. It is not certain whether these passages in Deuteronomy detail extra tithes (so there would be one tithe for the Levites, a second tithe for a celebratory meal, and a third tithe every three years for the poor) or whether they are different aspects of the one tithe.

2 Chronicles 31:5–12 describes how the tithe was brought into Jerusalem in the time of Hezekiah. As part of the promise made in Nehemiah's time, the people bound themselves to bring for the Levites the tithe into the storehouse (Nehemiah 10:37–8). Storekeepers were appointed to receive these tithes (Nehemiah 12:44). One of the storehouses for the tithe was taken over by Tobiah (Nehemiah 13:5). When he was thrown out, the tithe could be brought into the storehouse once more (Nehemiah 13:12).

Samuel warns the people that a king is likely to demand a tithe from them (1 Samuel 8:15, 17). This would be in addition to any tithes which were required by the Law.

In Malachi there is an injunction which is much used by the proponents of New Testament tithing, so we should quote it in full here (Malachi 3:8–10):

'Will a man rob God? Yet you rob me. But you ask, "How do we rob you?" In tithes and offerings. You are under a curse—the whole nation of you—because you are robbing me. Bring the whole tithe into the storehouse, that there may be food in my house. Test me in this,' says the Lord Almighty, 'and see if I will not throw open the floodgates of heaven and pour out so much blessing that you will not have room enough for it.'

I believe this is the entire stock of Old Testament references to the tithe. As you can see, the subject was very infrequently mentioned even before Christ's coming. It was, however, an integral part of the support of the Levites and the temple worship.

Tithing in the New Testament
If there are few references to tithing in the Old Testament, there are even fewer in the New. We will now consider all of these in turn.

In Hebrews 7:1–10 the writer points out that Abraham gave a tenth of everything to Melchizedek priest of Salem. This passage shows that Christ, of whom Melchizedek is a picture, is greater than Abraham. The less important person pays tithes to the more important. In no way does the passage suggest that tithing is something we must do.

Luke 18:12 describes the self-righteous Pharisee praying in the temple: 'I fast twice a week and give a tenth of all I get.' In Christ's eyes this man is worse than the tax collector who cries to God as a sinner for mercy (v. 13), and who is more likely to go home 'justified before God' (v. 14). Once again, there is nothing here to commend tithing as a practice we must follow.

In Matthew 23:23 (almost identical to Luke 11:42) Jesus chides the scribes and Pharisees for concentrating on tiny literal details of the law and neglecting weightier matters (the Luke verse specifies 'justice and the love of God'): 'You give a tenth of your spices—mint, dill and cummin. But you have neglected the more important matters of the law—justice, mercy and faithfulness. You should have practised the latter, without neglecting the former.'

Of all these four passages, only Matthew 23:23 and Luke 11:42 may be considered as in any way encouraging tithing. Christ declares that these people should have followed the important principles of the Law, but at the same time not neglected tithing their garden herbs. Should not the same apply to us?

However, Christ is here speaking to those who keep the Law. He is pointing out that such people cannot pick and choose, but must keep it all. They certainly must not tithe herbs whilst neglecting the weightier issues in the law, such as their attitude to God and their fellow man.

In these verses, does Christ make tithing obligatory for Christians? If so, then we have a problem. As we have seen, the Law is a unitary whole. Christ pronounced several parts of the Law as about to be repealed (the food laws and the half-shekel tax, for instance). Does it then seem reasonable that Christ should remove from us all the requirements of the Law except for that concerning the tithe?

If the whole of the New Testament teaching which encourages tithing lies in these two references, then we have to ask, 'Why is there so little evidence?' This would not be so bad if the evidence were clear-cut, but as we have seen it is not.

The assertions

Various assertions are made by those who support tithing for Christians. These will be examined here in turn.

(a) Christians must give 10% of their income

This is viewed as a necessity, stemming from the law of tithing in the Old Testament. Advocates of tithing appear to go to some lengths to avoid describing this as a legal requirement. They do, however, indicate that it is mandatory for Christians to tithe. As the issue is one which is laid down in the Law, it is hard to escape the conclusion that they are saying this is a part of the Law which we must keep. They also use Malachi 3:8-10 (quoted above) in support of this claim. These verses cover tithing in the context of keeping the Law. However, as we saw in the previous chapter, Christians are not under the Law. Nor are they under any part of the Law. To make them subject to part of the Law is to put them under the whole Law, which, as we have seen, is contrary to New Testament teaching. From this, does it seem likely that tithing should be an obligatory requirement for Christians?

Some have pointed out that if those under the Law had to give 10%, should we who are under grace not match this? There is much to be said for such an attitude. Christians should be generous. It is good to check just how much you are giving. An aim such as that of giving a tenth is something which can help you personally in self-discipline. But the whole point is this. It is perfectly fine to adopt such an aim voluntarily. It is another matter altogether to be under a need to keep part of the Law.

(b) Tithing precedes the Law and so is binding on us

Tithing is described in Genesis 14, long before the Law was given to Moses, and therefore, it is claimed, tithing has an origin and an importance which is not linked with the Law. However, circumcision was also introduced (in Genesis 17) well before it found a place in the Law, yet we have seen how circumcision for Christians is regarded in the New Testament. The believer who for religious reasons receives circumcision is 'alienated from Christ' (Galatians 5:4). Is there not similarly a spiritual danger for those who consider that one must keep the rules about tithing? It is true that tithing precedes the Law, but that does not mean it is binding on us, any more than circumcision.

(c) The tithe must be given to the local church

It is asserted that 'storehouse' in Malachi 3:10 is to be interpreted for us as 'one's local church' and nothing else. This is certainly an audacious claim. Originally, Malachi was obviously referring to the place within the temple where the tithe was stored. It was a tithe in kind (the produce of the land), and so a place was needed to store it until it could be used. It may have a figurative interpretation also, but if it does, we would need to know why it should be interpreted in that particular way. The New Testament gives us no hint that the local church is a 'storehouse'. In fact, the New Testament says little or nothing about giving anything for the local church, as we will see later in this chapter. The very absence of evidence in the New Testament linking the 'storehouse' to the local church may in itself be taken as evidence against such a link.

(d) The blessing of Malachi 3:10 is available to those who tithe
As we saw in the previous chapter, the Law is associated with blessings and curses. The whole Law included the blessings and curses of Deuteronomy chapters 27 and 28. It is true that Malachi 3:10 includes the promise that God will 'throw open the floodgates of heaven and pour out so much blessing that you will not have room enough for it'. However, verse 9 shows the corresponding curse: 'You are under a curse ... because you are robbing me.'

Beware of the blessings of the Law; a curse is not far away. 'Christ redeemed us from the curse of the law by becoming a curse for us' (Galatians 3:13). We have died to the Law, to both its curses and its blessings. God now blesses us in Christ with every spiritual blessing (Ephesians 1:3), and we do not need to put ourselves under the Law to gain any other blessing.

The missing evidence
If it is true that believers have an obligation to tithe their income and give it to the local church, we would expect to find mention of this requirement somewhere in the New Testament. Why is this evidence missing? Would tithing pass the desert island test mentioned in Chapter 2?

It has been suggested that any mention of tithing was not necessary because it was 'so deeply imbedded in the Jewish conscience' (Kendall's words). Converted Jews, it is supposed, would naturally tithe. However, this does not explain why no teaching on this subject is given to Gentile converts for whom it was not customary. Even for Jews there would need to be teaching to explain why the tithe no longer should be given to the Levites but rather to the local church. As described above, there were three different applications of the tithe (or else three different tithes), which are now apparently to be replaced by one tithe. How would they understand these things without clear instructions? Why would tithing still be necessary if the half-shekel tax, so vital a part of Jewish life, is now defunct?

One thing was indeed 'deeply imbedded in the Jewish conscience': the need to keep the Law. It is because of this that the New Testament gives much teaching to explain how this has been superseded. If we are now to consider ourselves dead to the Law as a whole, and yet the law on tithing still applied to us, this would surely need to be mentioned.

In Acts 15 the apostles met together to discuss whether converted Gentiles should be taught to keep the Law of Moses. The matters enjoined on such believers (v. 20) (which seem to be those needed to avoid offending Jews) do not include tithing. Would this not have been the ideal place to include such a regulation? If they needed to be taught of the need to avoid eating blood, certainly a matter 'deeply embedded in the Jewish conscience', they would obviously need to be taught about tithing also.

Galatians 2:1–10 records how Paul agreed with Peter, James and John as to the gospel, and how Paul was to present it to the Gentiles. The one point which the apostles to the circumcised insisted on was not that the Gentiles should be taught to tithe, but that they should be taught to remember the poor (v.10).

Paul in 1 Corinthians 16:2 recommends every reader to give 'in keeping with his income'. If Paul wanted to emphasise the need to give one tenth of one's income, this would surely have been the ideal place to state it. However, Paul does not specify the rate of giving, but merely makes it relative to one's prosperity in general.

Christian giving

The New Testament is one with the Old in stressing the need for generosity in giving. This is especially so in 2 Corinthians chapters 8 and 9. The reason why we need to be generous is because this is exactly what God is like, and we are to be imitators of God. Our Lord Jesus Christ was rich, but for our sakes became poor, that we through his poverty might become rich (8:9). God gave us an indescribable gift when he gave us his Son (9:15). Our giving should primarily be of ourselves to the Lord (8:5).

In the New Testament giving is not spoken of as being for the local church, but rather for individuals in need. Sometimes this money is brought to the church for later distribution. In Acts there was sacrificial giving, people selling fields and property (Acts 4:34–7). The money was given to the apostles for distribution to needy believers (Acts 5:35; 6:1), a task which the apostles soon delegated to the seven (Acts 6:1–6). Apparently the churches later enrolled destitute widows as those to be supported financially (1 Timothy 5:3–16, especially v. 16). Elders who preached and taught well were to be given a 'double honour', i.e. a full remuneration (1 Timothy 5:17). Paul on his missionary journeys was sent financial help by the Philippians (Philippians 4:14–19).

Most stress is laid on the need for giving to the poor of the Jerusalem church. This is in fact the subject of 2 Corinthians chapters 8 and 9. The principle laid down there is that among believers we should aim for financial levelling-up (8:14). Paul's comments in 1 Corinthians 16:1–4, about laying something aside on the first day of every week, are not directed to giving for the local church but rather giving for poor believers at Jerusalem.

In all of this, there is no mention about the needs of the local church as such. Nor is any mention made of giving a tithe. This is not to say that in our modern world a Christian has no responsibility for the expenses incurred by his own church. It is a disgrace and shame for us not to provide adequately for our own spiritual home and those who serve in it. However, those who affirm that 10% of income must be given to the local church can find little backing for this view from the New Testament

All our money belongs to the Lord. 2 Corinthians 9:7 provides a clear commentary on Christian giving: 'Each man should give what he has decided in his heart to give, not reluctantly or under compulsion, for God loves a cheerful giver.'

Each one is to make up his or her mind what to give, and should not be compelled to give a certain amount. We are not to be under compulsion from other Christians or from the Law. If a Christian is to decide to give a tenth because he or she wants to do at least as much as people did in the Old Testament, then that is their personal choice. Our giving should be characterised by willingness, generosity and joy.

Above all, our giving should be a thank-offering to God who has freed us from the condemnation of sin and the Law and has put his Spirit in our hearts. Giving should not be subject to the petty-mindedness of legal regulations (gross or net, weekly or monthly?) but from hearts that have been won by love, fulfilling the Law in the only way in which it can be truly fulfilled, by love in return.

In conclusion

This is indeed a strange situation. Some evangelical leaders, thoroughly convinced that the Bible is the inspired word of God, are strong in their support for a matter for which the scriptures provide little or no evidence.

Loving, caring pastors bring their flock into condemnation if they do not follow legalistic precepts. What can be the explanation?

Perhaps behind this insistence on the need for tithing to the local church is the structure of the church. The local church has such need for funds because of the way it operates. Often the kinds of churches which have been set up need a great deal of money for their upkeep and maintenance. We will return to this matter in a later chapter.

From what has been covered in previous chapters, it seems quite unacceptable to declare that any Christian *must* fulfil a requirement of the Law. We are not accepted by God on the basis of our fulfilment of the Law, nor do blessings from God come by our observance of the Law. We have died to the Law.

On the other hand, Christians should generously support those in need. Our own churches should not be deprived of our financial assistance. If someone decides that giving 10% of their income to their local church is a useful guide, then that is what they should give, not because they are compelled to do this, but because they choose to do so.

And finally . . .
Some believe that in Matthew 23:23 (and Luke 11:42) Jesus is instructing us to continue tithing. Such people do not seem really to apply these words as they are written. Christ is not just encouraging you to give a tenth of your income: apparently he is specifying the need to tithe every shoot of mint which grows up in your garden. Have you thought of that?

9

The Sabbath

Two men, A and B, were talking together after the morning service. (This is a true story, but I will not say which denomination it was to which they belonged.) A was showing B the car he had for sale. The following conversation took place:

B: *Now, if this wasn't a Sunday, and if I asked you how much you were wanting for the car, what would you say?*

A: *Well, if this wasn't a Sunday, and you asked me how much I was wanting for the car, I would say . . .*

B: *Now, if this wasn't a Sunday and you told me you were wanting . . . for the car, and I offered you . . . what would you say?*

And so the bargaining continued until a satisfactory figure was reached, each man happy with a business deal completed and yet the Sabbath left unviolated.

Does each Christian really have to keep Sunday in the same way that Israel of old had to keep the Sabbath? Do we also need to ensure that our society as a whole respects Sunday, and calls a halt to trade, planes, trains, ferries etc? This chapter sets out to investigate the way the Sabbath is presented throughout the Bible, ending up with its position in the New Testament, and to trace the lessons for us today.

The Sabbath in the Old Testament

The Sabbath originates at the start of the Bible, when the creation is described as taking place over six days. 'On the seventh day God rested from all his work,' we are told (Genesis 2:2). 'And God blessed the seventh day and made it holy' (v. 3).

Keeping the Sabbath was included as the fourth of the ten commandments: 'Remember the Sabbath day by keeping it holy' (Exodus 20:8). The reason for the Sabbath was that 'in six days the Lord made the heavens and the earth, the sea, and all that is in them, but he rested on the seventh day. Therefore the Lord blessed the Sabbath day and made it holy' (v. 8).

The Sabbath was principally a day of rest, one in seven. On the Sabbath day no fire was to be kindled in houses (Exodus 35:3); nor sticks gathered (Numbers 15:32–6); nor burdens carried (Nehemiah 13:19; Jeremiah 17:22, 24, 27). Buying or selling were prohibited (Nehemiah 10:31). Those who violated the Sabbath were to be put to death (Exodus 31:15; Numbers 15:35).

The Sabbath was more than a mere cessation of work. It was to be God's day, a day holy to (set apart for) the Lord (Jeremiah 17:21, 24, 27; Ezekiel 20:20; 44:24). Every Sabbath the showbread was set out afresh in the tabernacle or temple (Leviticus 24:8). Two extra lambs were sacrificed (Numbers 28:9–10). In Ezekiel's vision of the new temple the people were to worship at the gate each Sabbath (Ezek. 46:3).

Isaiah has much to say about the way the Sabbath should be observed as a holy day for the Lord: 'If you keep your feet from breaking the Sabbath and from doing as you please on my holy day, if you call the Sabbath a delight and the Lord's holy day honourable, and if you honour it by not going your own way and not doing as you please or speaking idle words, then you will find your joy in the Lord' (Isaiah 58:13–14).

The Sabbath was a sign that the people were the Lord's and that he would make them holy (Exodus 31:13; Ezekiel 20:12, 20). When the Jews failed to keep the Law, including the Sabbath, one purpose fulfilled by them being exiled to Babylon was that 'the land enjoyed its Sabbath rests' (2 Chronicles 36:21).

Since we are no longer under the Law, we should not necessarily expect that observance of the Sabbath applies to us as it did to Israel.

The Sabbath in the New Testament

In the New Testament we find that a traditional custom had become established for Jews on the Sabbath. This custom, followed both by Jesus and Paul, was to go to the synagogue (Matthew 12:9; Acts 13:14; 17:1–2; 18:4), where the Old Testament would be read (Luke 4:16–20; Acts 13:15, 27; 15:21) and expounded (Luke 4:21–7) and teaching given (Mark 1:21; 6:2; Luke 4:31; 6:6; 13:10; Acts 13:15).

It is in the nature of legalism to specify and measure the limits of the laws. So the Jews had defined how far one might travel on the Sabbath—the Sabbath day's journey (Acts 1:12). By New Testament times the Sabbath had become one of the laws about which the Jews were most keen.

Christ encountered some of the fiercest opposition against himself when the Jews accused him of not keeping the Sabbath. There was, for instance, the time when he and his disciples went through a grainfield on the Sabbath (Matthew 12:1–8; Mark 2:23–8; Luke 6:1–5). His disciples plucked grain and rubbed the seeds in their hands to remove chaff, operations which were seen as harvesting and threshing, activities which were not permitted on the Sabbath. Many times he healed on the Sabbath, despite the protests of those who claimed it was not lawful (Matthew 12:10–14; Mark 3:1–5; Luke

6:6–10; 13:11–16; 14:2–6; John 5:2–16; 7:22–3; 9:14–16). His defence was two-fold. On the one hand he pointed out that 'The Sabbath was made for man, not man for the Sabbath' (Mark 2:27). On the other hand, he claimed that 'The Son of Man is Lord of the Sabbath' (Matthew 12:8; Mark 2:28; Luke 6:5). It was for him to determine how the Sabbath should be kept.

God's Sabbath rest

We have seen so far in this book several cases where the Old Testament teaches literal truth which is transformed in the New Testament into spiritual truth. The literal events in the Old are taken in the New as pictures of the spiritual reality into which we now enter. Paul tells us: 'Do not let anyone judge you by what you eat or drink, or with regard to . . . a Sabbath day. These are a shadow of the things that were to come; the reality, however, is found in Christ' (Colossians 2:16–17). So we can expect to find an explanation in the New Testament of the reality which is pictured by the Old Testament Sabbath.

The New Testament has radical teaching concerning God's rest day, which we have seen from Genesis 2:2 was the day following his creation of the universe. When Jesus was persecuted for healing on the Sabbath, he said 'My Father is always at his work to this very day, and I, too, am working' (John 5:17–18). The import of Jesus' words here needs to be carefully followed. What he seems to be saying is:
1. This current age is the time of God's Sabbath;
2. Despite this, God is still at work in this day and age;
3. If God can work during the age of his Sabbath, Jesus can heal on the Sabbath day.

If this interpretation is correct, then it opens up other questions. If this present age is God's day of rest, then perhaps the six days described in Genesis 1 might also be not literal days of 24 hours but ages. Are we justified in bending the word 'day' to such an extent?

One problem with literal interpretations is that words will sometimes not keep still enough for us to pin them down literally. The word 'day', for instance, may be used to mean 12 hours (Genesis 1:5), 24 hours (Exodus 20:10), or may span a whole week: 'The day the Lord God made the earth and the heavens' (Genesis 2:4 Hebrew). There are many references in the Bible to 'the day of the Lord', but it is hard to say that a day of 24 hours is meant. It is surely not surprising that God's time does not necessarily parallel ours. After all, Peter reminds us that 'with the Lord a day is like a thousand years' (2 Peter 3:8).

Some may object to making the days of creation into epochs. After all, in the ten commandments, the requirement to keep holy one day in seven is linked to the fact that God took six days over creation and rested on the seventh (Exodus 20:9-11). So God's seven days of creation are made the reason for us resting one day in seven, therefore, so it is said, God's seven days are of the same duration as our days.

However, one could interpret the verses in Exodus 20 as follows. God set the pattern of work and rest by working for six 'cosmic' days then resting on the seventh. This pattern is to be followed by Israel working for six earthly days and resting on the seventh. We need not be surprised if God's clock does not run to the same time as ours.

A friend of mine was listening to a cricket match on the radio. This was being played at Lord's cricket ground, north London. He was electrified when the commentator said, 'It's now five to twelve by the Lord's clock.' Perhaps the commentator's words were truer than he realised!

The interpretation which I have presented here may seem very strange to those who have been brought up to see things very differently and quite literally. More light may be shed on this matter as we see more of what the New Testament says about the relation of God's Sabbath rest to us.

Entering God's Sabbath rest

The writer to the Hebrews has much to say on the subject of Sabbath rest. He speaks of some individuals being able to enter God's Sabbath, and others who failed to enter.

He quotes Psalm 95, in which God says of the Israelites who rebelled when they came out of Egypt, 'They shall never enter my rest' (Hebrews 3:11). In chapter 4 the writer exhorts his readers to take the promise of entering into God's rest. When Joshua took the people into the promised land, they did not enter into the fulness of rest which God intended (v. 8). The rest about which he speaks is God's Sabbath rest, which believers enter into: 'We who have believed enter that rest, just as God has said, "So I declared on oath in my anger, 'They shall never enter my rest.' " And yet his work has been finished since the creation of the world. For somewhere he has spoken about the seventh day in these words: "And on the seventh day God rested from all his work" ' (Hebrews 4:3–4).

The truth which the writer to the Hebrews is seeking to convey is this. Because God finished his works at the foundation of the world, it has been possible to enter into God's rest ever since that time. This is the age of God's Sabbath which his people may share in: 'There remains, then, a Sabbath-rest for the people of God; for anyone who enters God's rest also rests from his own work, just as God did from his' (Hebrews 4:9–10).

For people, the Sabbath is a day of rest at the end of the week. For God, however, the Sabbath during which he rests is this present age. Just as he ceased from his work when the world was finished, so those who trust in Christ cease from trying to earn salvation by their own efforts, and accept by faith what God gives.

The Lord's day
The Sabbath was the seventh day of the week, or Saturday. The day which Christians have observed as special throughout the ages is, of course, the first day of the week, Sunday.

The first day of the week is the day on which Christ rose from the dead (Matt. 28:1; Mark 16:2, 9; Luke 24:1; John 20:1, 19). In Troas it is recorded that on the first day of the week the believers gathered to break bread (i.e. to eat the communion meal) (Acts 20:7). Contributions for believers suffering hardship were to be laid aside (presumably into the church treasury) 'on the first day of every week' (1 Corinthians 16:2), leading us to suppose that the church met then. However, it is not to be supposed that Christians necessarily had a day of rest then. Some of them were slaves and would not be allowed a day off. This is perhaps why in Acts 20:7 it appears that they met late at night, and so Paul 'kept on talking until midnight'.

The only specific reference to 'the Lord's day' in the New Testament is Revelation 1:10, where John tells us, 'On the Lord's Day I was in the Spirit'. This can only mean the day when the Lord rose from the dead, i.e. Sunday, the first day of the week.

From such slight references a large tradition has grown. It has always been the custom for Christians to meet on Sunday. Some have even referred to Sunday as 'the Sabbath'. The idea has developed in some circles that it is wrong for us to do any laborious work on this day, or indeed to cause others to perform undue work. One's best clothes are worn on this day. In earlier times children were restricted in their play on Sundays, and were given special toys for this day only. Old Testament scriptures which referred to the Sabbath were invoked as applying to Sundays. In other words, Sunday observance has replaced Sabbath observance as a law enjoined on us.

The New Testament never commands us to keep the Lord's Day, to make it holy. We need to beware lest, having exchanged the restrictions of the Law for the freedom of the gospel, we proceed to make fresh laws out of the gospel freedom.

'It is for freedom that Christ has set us free. Stand firm, then, and do not let yourselves be burdened again by a yoke of slavery' (Galatians 5:1). We are free in Christ. We are free to meet together on a Sunday if that is what we wish. We are free not to do this, if we would rather meet together on another day. We are free from bondage to the Law, including the law about the Sabbath.

Conclusions

The provision of one day in seven for rest and refreshment is a necessary one. God knows what is best for our human bodies and minds, and we neglect this provision to our cost. Employers who care for their workers' welfare will ensure that they are able to spend time in recreation and enjoying their families. As Jesus said, 'The sabbath was made for man' (Mark 2:27).

So long as Christians continue to meet on a Sunday, it is beneficial for believers to have this as their day off so that they can have fellowship. This is not always possible for those in certain occupations, but good employers will allow their workers to have this day free if they so wish.

As Christians, we must ensure that we do not lose our freedom from the Law. If we are not careful, tradition will saddle us with restrictions. We will be faced with deciding what is permissible on a Sunday and what is not. Such petty decisions are the hallmark of legalism. Every day of the week we are to enjoy the Sabbath rest of reconciliation and peace with God, which does not depend on our works.

And finally . . .

To this day the Jewish Sabbath has been from sunset on Friday until sunset on Saturday. You can see the effect of this in Mark 1:32. So as not to break the Law, the people waited during the Sabbath and only brought the sick to Jesus after sunset. If Christians are to keep the first day of the week as once the Jews kept the seventh day, should they not start the Lord's Day at sunset on Saturday, and finish it at sunset on the Sunday? Have you thought of that?

10

The Bible and science

Our very young daughter was puzzled. 'I can't believe my eyes!' she exclaimed. 'I can only believe my toes!' She was experimenting with words, of course, as children will. But have you considered what a predicament we would be in if we could not believe what our eyes tell us? The world around us would be nothing but a web of deception.

This chapter is very much about believing our eyes. How much can we trust the evidence of our senses? What picture of the world do they present us with?

There are people whose work entails using their eyes to investigate the kind of world in which we live. They are, of course, scientists. Much has been written about the conflict between science and faith. It is unfortunate that there has been such a bitter opposition between those exploring the creation of God and those exploring the God of creation. There has been distrust on both sides, but especially on the part of Christians who have found themselves with their backs to the wall, apparently dreading each new discovery, and ready to contest scientific findings as if they were the work of the enemy.

Truth is not two-faced; it is consistent and does not lie. It is not seemly for scientists and Bible students each to try to pull things their own way like bedfellows pulling the blankets off one another. It is my hope here that I might help Christians to understand the way scientists work, and to see that there need not be such conflict between science and the Bible.

The surprising thing is that such a state of affairs should have come about. In past centuries many of the leading scientists were committed Christians.

Michael Faraday, an experimenter who made pioneer discoveries on the relation between electricity and magnetism, was a faithful member of a Bible-believing group, the Sandemanians, and testified of his own relationship to Christ.

James Clerk Maxwell, a brilliant theoretician who formulated the laws of electromagnetism, surrendered his life to Christ as Saviour whilst a student and spent hours reading his Bible.

Lord Kelvin, a developer of the Second Law of Thermodynamics, whose name is now immortalised in the absolute temperature scale, had a personal faith in Christ based on the Bible, which was his pillar throughout life.

Sir James Young Simpson, who discovered chloroform, was once asked what his greatest discovery was. 'When I discovered Jesus Christ as my personal Saviour,' was his reply.

So the list could go on. There are many scientists today who make no secret of their faith in Christ. 'The heavens declare the glory of God; the skies proclaim the work of his hands,' declares David (Psalm 19:1). There can surely be nothing wrong in exploring the heavens and the earth and thereby tracing God's handiwork. In fact, rightly understood, these things point to God the Creator (Romans 1:20).

Scientific method

Scientists work according to certain principles which need to be understood before we criticise their findings. This is to some extent the 'basis of faith' for scientists, and needs to be taken on trust by those setting out on a scientific career.

Scientists for the most part believe (though they cannot prove it) that the universe is **rational** and **homogeneous**. The universe is supposed to be rational in that it works according to certain fixed laws which are there to be discovered. It is supposed to be homogeneous in that the laws work the same for all time and in all places. Without such assumptions the work of scientific discovery would be well nigh impossible. Christians will presumably have no difficulty accepting these assumptions, because this is the way that a God of order and reason would be expected to work.

The method normally followed by all scientists is in two parts. The first part is to gather data which provide evidence of how nature works. The other part is to seek to condense the data into laws which adequately describe them. So the two parts of this process are (a) gathering data and (b) formulating laws. The laws should be as simple as possible, and yet describe the data fully. Sometimes a law is thought of first, and experiments are then carried out to see whether data can be found to substantiate it. Sometimes the data are found first, and a law is then sought to explain them. Often the two processes of data-gathering and the formulation of laws go hand in hand.

A law is sometimes referred to as a theory, but there does not seem to be a consistent use of the terms 'theory' and 'law'. One should not suppose that because a certain idea is termed a 'theory' that it is any less firmly held by scientists than a 'law'.

Any law which is postulated should be **testable**. It should be possible to carry out once again the experiments which appeared to support this law, and when these experiments are repeated they should yield the same results.

It should also be possible to carry out further experiments, which will show whether or not the law is still applicable under new conditions. The law should be **productive** in the sense that it should suggest new tests which could be carried out which will confirm or deny the validity of the law.

A law should preferably be expressed in **mathematical** terms. Mathematics is the handmaid of science, and scientific laws may most conveniently be represented by mathematical formulae. This need was expressed by Roger Bacon (c. 1220 - c. 1292), who was not only a scientist but also a Franciscan Friar.

One thing which Christians sometimes find hard to understand is that the 'laws' of science are not fixed and unchangeable. A law may cover certain data, but further experiments may highlight data which the law does not explain. Then a new law needs to be drawn up, and the old law revised or abandoned. This is the nature of science. It should be possible to prove any law to be false, given the right evidence. Scientists being as they are, human like the rest of us, there is sometimes great reluctance to abandon an old law for a new one, despite the evidence which is amassed to show that this is needed. However, true science should always be ready to change in order to be true to the data.

False science tries to uphold a certain viewpoint irrespective of the facts; true science is always open to the truth. As Christians we ought to honour such an aim. In handling the Bible we also should follow the same desire for truth rather than to justify and preserve our interpretations or traditions in the face of much contrary evidence.

An example

An example might serve to show how scientists have investigated events, accumulated evidence, formulated laws which cover the evidence, and then revised the laws.

Over the centuries people observed the sun, moon and stars. The sun appeared to rotate round the earth once per day. Some stars (the 'fixed stars') appeared to rotate round the earth almost once per day, but the sun moved past them over a one-year period. The moon also appeared to rotate round the earth once per day, but shifted its position and appearance over a four-week period. Some 'stars' had a more peculiar motion, sometimes almost travelling with the sun and other stars, and at other times moving backwards or forwards against the background of stars. These were called 'planets', meaning 'wanderers'.

The law which they constructed to explain the data was as follows. They supposed that the earth was surrounded with various transparent spheres to which the heavenly bodies were attached. These spheres rotated round the earth at different speeds. The fixed stars were attached to the outermost sphere, and the moon was attached to a smaller sphere which rotated slightly faster. The earth was at the centre of these spheres.

And what about the planets? This was a much harder matter. It was believed that only perfect entities were fitting for the heavens. (Note that this was a part of scientific method at the time which was later abandoned.) Spheres are perfect, so any explanation must be in terms of spheres. The theory was therefore modified for the planets. The basic sphere for any planet had, at one point on its surface, another sphere, also rotating. This second sphere may have another sphere attached to it, and so on. The planet was situated on the surface of one of the subsidiary spheres. With the right diameters and speeds of rotation for each sphere, the motion of the planet could be described. This was the theory propounded by Ptolemy in the 2nd century AD, and so was known as the Ptolemaic theory.

It was, however, a very cumbersome description. It was partly necessitated by the views that (a) everything rotated round the earth and that (b) only spheres were suited to the explanation. As more detailed information on the motions of the planets came to hand, yet more spheres attached to spheres attached to spheres had to be postulated.

In 1543 Copernicus published his theory that the planets rotated around the sun, and so did the earth. The earth rotated on its axis once every 24 hours, which made it appear that everything in the heavens was rotating round the earth. This theory made the description of the universe very much simpler. Galileo helped to confirm this theory when in 1610 he saw four moons orbiting Jupiter. So not everything rotated round the earth after all.

Further investigation modified the Copernican theory and built on it. Kepler showed that the planets did not travel in circles, but in ellipses. Newton formulated the laws of gravitation which underpinned such motion.

Einstein showed that Newton's laws of motion and gravitation were only approximate, and replaced them with the laws of relativity which covered phenomena which Newton's laws could not explain. Newton's laws of gravitation in particular were eventually superseded by Einstein's General Theory of Relativity. This also replaced Newton's concept of bodies attracting one another by inexplicable action at a distance. Instead, massive bodies were supposed to cause distortions in space-time, and other bodies were deflected in their paths by these distortions.

The result has been a succession of theories or laws, each one describing observed data which the one before could not. Sometimes this has been achieved by means of a simpler law; sometimes the newcomer has been much more complicated. However, the whole process has been one motivated by the desire to discover the truth and to formulate the laws which the created universe obeys. Those of us who believe in a creator God must surely believe that these are (at least approximations to) the laws which he laid down. Scientists have sometimes considered their task as 'thinking God's thoughts after him'.

The sun stood still
Before we tackle the thorny subjects of creation and evolution, we will consider a passage from which there is much to learn, and which has been in the past a battleground between scientists and Christians.

The passage concerns Joshua's attack on the nations assaulting Israel's ally, Gibeon (Joshua 10:12–14). When Joshua was pursuing the fleeing Amorites, he prayed, 'O sun, stand still' (v. 12). The record continues, 'So the sun stood still' (v. 13).

How are we to interpret this passage? If we apply the principles of Chapter 2, we see that this is a descriptive passage in the middle of a book which sets out to be historical. God answered Joshua's prayer and intervened with a miracle which lengthened by one day the time which Israel had for effectively pursuing their enemies. We have no reason to accept these verses as other than describing an actual physical event. But what was that event?

Various possibilities have been advanced. If the earth stopped rotating, everyone on it would have been flung forward at a speed of several hundred miles per hour, and the effect on the oceans would be to produce a tsunami which would make the Amorites the least of Joshua's worries. Darkness lasting 24 hours (the sun not appearing) would hardly assist the pursuit, though a hailstorm (v. 11) would certainly imply heavy clouds and diminished light.

I have to say that I do not know how to interpret this passage. One of the principles suggested at the end of Chapter 2 was 'Be prepared to admit your ignorance.' Well, at this point I am admitting mine. We then have to ask, 'How much does it matter?' The way in which God performed a miracle lasting 24 hours does not really make much difference to us.

There is, however, something which makes a profound difference. Some have said that these verses prove that the sun rotates round the earth, and not the other way around. This is a statement, not about the miracle lasting 24 hours, but about our everyday situation.

The Copernican theory was published a few years before the death of Martin Luther. When Luther was told about the theory, his immediate reaction was that it could not be correct, because Joshua had commanded the sun to stand still, and so it must be the sun that moves.

One of the principles outlined in Chapter 2 was 'Consider the context of the world around us'. An examination of the world has led to the conclusion that the sun does not go round the earth each day. Since the time that Ptolemaic theory was current, we have discovered that there are stars and galaxies at extreme distances from the earth. If we reverted to that theory, we would now be faced with the problem of all these stars and galaxies travelling round the earth once every day.

Earlier in this chapter we described how scientists believe that the universe is rational, working according to laws which may be discovered and described mathematically. This basis of science seems just what we would expect if the universe had been created by a rational God, so it seems that this basis should be readily accepted by Christians.

Modern theories of cosmology are based on testable laws such as gravitation (or General Relativity), which are now well-established. The simplest explanation according to these laws is that the earth (which is lighter) rotates around the sun (which is much more massive). If the whole universe revolved around the earth once per day, we would have no such laws to explain the forces acting on far distant bodies travelling round us at such speeds. The universe would appear to be a nonsense.

Even though we may be convinced that the apparent motion of the sun is in fact due to the earth's rotation, we still speak about 'sunrise' and 'sunset'. We would be extremely pedantic to talk of 'that time when, due to the earth's rotation, we are first able to see the sun above the eastern horizon'. 'Sunrise' is a much simpler term. Similarly, when we travel fast in a vehicle we may refer to things outside 'speeding by us'. This is not to say that we consider that we are still and the whole world is moving past us. It is simply that language is very often used in this way.

I suggest that in the passage in Joshua language is being used in a similar way. Would it be sensible to turn the whole universe inside-out and upside-down simply because of the words used in this verse?

Conclusion first, evidence later

The principle 'Consider the context of the world around us' means that, when you are seeking to interpret a Bible verse, you need to consider also what the world around you is like. The trouble is that some Christians turn this the other way round. When seeking to find out what the world is like, they consider first what the Bible says, or rather, what they think the Bible says. Usually it is a case of imposing a literal interpretation of the Bible on the world around. The universe, they conclude, was made in six literal days. It is no more than a few thousand years old.

Having come to such conclusions based on their interpretation of the Bible, how are they to deal with the evidence which is continually being discovered? One size of shoe will fit all feet provided that you are prepared to push hard enough. Evidence must be forced to fit the conclusions already arrived at, instead of letting the evidence speak for itself. The impression is 'My mind is made up: don't confuse me with facts.'

This highlights the difference between the scientific approach (gathering data which provide evidence of how nature works and condensing the data into laws which adequately describe them) and the 'creationist' approach (arriving at a conclusion based on a literal interpretation of the Bible and then seeking to show that all data fits this conclusion).

The latter may result in a refusal to believe the evidence of one's eyes. In seeking to give the highest credit to the Bible by interpreting it ultra-literally we may be in danger of bringing discredit on God for creating an anarchic universe.

The creation

You may not have any difficulty in accepting that the earth rotates around itself once per day, which gives rise to the false impression that everything rotates round the earth. However, what has been said about 'the sun standing still' in Joshua 10 will serve as an introduction to more difficult matters where the Bible appears to clash with science in sharper ways.

The subject of the creation of the world has become a highly contentious one for Christians. You may not be convinced by what I present here. The decision as to what you believe is, of course, entirely yours. All I ask is that you hear my arguments, so that you may at least understand how some Bible-believing Christians arrive at their conclusions. One thing I want to make very certain. I personally believe that God created the universe and all it contains. It seems to me a pity that those who hold one particular view of the way creation happened should have cornered the term 'creationist'. I may not share those views, but that does not prevent me from being a 'creationist' in the wider sense of the term.

The scientific standpoint on the origin of the universe has been confirmed by increasing evidence over the years. We look out on our own galaxy, the Milky Way, containing around 100 billion stars (of which our Sun is one). The Milky Way is about 100,000 light years in diameter. (A light year is the distance which light travels in one year, and is 5,880 billion miles, or 9,440 billion kilometres). Many other galaxies may be seen, some of them billions of light years away. There may be more than 100 billion galaxies in total.

One fact has become apparent for astronomers. The further galaxies are from us, the faster they are travelling away from us. This does not mean that we are in the centre of the universe. Imagine a balloon with spots on it being blown up. As the balloon gets bigger, the spots get further apart, although no one spot may be said to be at the centre of the movement. This kind of thing seems to be happening with the universe.

Now imagine winding time back, like a film which is projected backwards. The galaxies all rush towards one another. If this continued unchecked, there would be a time (in the past) when they were all competing for the same place.

This has led scientists to suppose that the universe began in a gigantic explosion which they call the 'Big Bang'. The best evidence so far points to an instant approximately 13.8 billion years ago. Since then everything in the universe has been flying apart. The more evidence which is accumulated, the surer scientists become that this is the way the universe began.

The age of the universe
Scientists and Bible-believing Christians alike believe that the universe has not always existed, but came into being at one instant. You would think that Christians would be glad that science has at last come to agree with them on this matter. Very often, they draw no comfort from the Big Bang. The differences are now no longer about a definite start for the universe, but about when it happened.

If a galaxy is estimated to be one billion light years away, then light from it has been travelling for one billion years before reaching us. We are seeing that galaxy not as it is now but as it was one billion years ago. So on the basis of this one galaxy the universe as a whole would seem to be at least one billion years old. As we have seen, scientists have been narrowing down their estimate of the time of the Big Bang. It seems now that 13.7 billion years ago is the most likely figure.

Some Christians are convinced that when Genesis chapter 1 speaks of a creation in six days, these must be taken literally as days of 24 hours duration. If this is so, then a necessary consequence is that the universe is not very old. By adding up the ages at which parents in the Bible had children, Archbishop Usher concluded that the earth was created in 4004 BC. Unfortunately, the ages as recorded in the Hebrew Bible differ from those in the Greek version of the Old Testament (the Septuagint). However, one would suppose that if the days in Genesis chapter 1 are indeed literal, the earth is not much more than, say, 10,000 years old.

Some have suggested that the earth was created just a few thousand years ago *looking as if* it were much older. We need to consider this idea closely. Let us suppose that the earth was in fact created 10,000 years ago. In that case, when we look out at the night sky, stars which are less than 10,000 light years away are truly there; we are seeing light which originated at those stars. In the case of stars which are further away, we are not seeing light from real stars, we are seeing light which was created 10,000 years ago *looking as if* it was coming from real stars.

You may have seen an advertisement, say, featuring bottles of perfume. These are in a regular array which appears to go back in the distance to infinity. However, on closer inspection you see that only the bottles in the foreground are real. The rest are painted on the backdrop. Is this what the universe is like?

Such an idea would certainly run counter to the scientist's assumption that the universe is homogeneous. Part of the universe would be real, and part an illusion. It would also deal a heavy blow to the idea that the universe is rational. We cannot believe the evidence of our eyes. The universe would then be so set up that when we consider the evidence we are led to the conclusion that the universe is very old, but this is just an illusion. Some might think that one could no longer say that 'The heavens declare the glory of God': it seems that the heavens represent the biggest fraud ever perpetrated.

A reconciliation

The Bible account of the creation and the scientist's description may easily be reconciled. When interpreting Genesis 1 we need to use the principle, 'Consider the context of the world around us.' In the light of that, we interpret the days not as periods of 24 hours, but as epochs.

Are we doing violence to Genesis 1 if we interpret it in this way? Let us look at that chapter in the light of the principles outlined in Chapter 2. In particular, let us consider the passage within the context of the rest of the book. From Genesis chapter 4 on to the end of the book the material is presented as a historical record of people, which we would expect to take as historical fact. The first three chapters are somewhat different. (This is not to say that they are any the less true.)

For one thing, we seem to have two different accounts of creation. Genesis 1:1–2:3 depicts creation in seven days, culminating in the creation of plants, animals and finally mankind, male and female. Genesis 2:4–25, on the other hand, describes the creation of Adam before any plants had appeared (v. 5), then the creation of the animals (vv. 19–20), then the creation of Eve (vv. 21–3).

Some have suggested that chapter 1 describes the creation in the universe at large, whereas chapter 2 covers what subsequently happened in the Garden of Eden. This seems less than satisfactory. God formed Adam just before he planted the garden (2:8). Creating mankind, male and female, first (in Genesis 1), and then creating Adam in the garden (in Genesis 2) would surely mean that many men and women would not be descendants of Adam and Eve, but would precede them.

I believe that both accounts of the creation are true. This must mean that one or other of them, or both, are to be interpreted figuratively in some respects. They appear to be showing us different aspects of God's creation. Perhaps chapter 1 is showing us the order in which things were created, and how man is the summit of that creation, whereas chapter 2 is showing us the inter-relations between parts of that creation, and how no animal can satisfactorily be man's partner in the way that his wife can.

We need to look at the beginning of Genesis in the light of the New Testament. We have seen in the previous chapter that the Sabbath appears in the New Testament (and even in Christ's words) as the current age. Could not the first six days of creation also be ages?

It appears that to interpret Genesis 1 in the light of ages rather than days does no violence to the Bible. If, on the other hand, we insist that the universe was created in six days of 24 hours, the violence which we do to our concept of a rational, homogeneous creation is devastating. My opinion on this is obvious. What is yours?

The Theory of Evolution

If there is one aspect of science which causes even more problems for Christians than creation it is the Theory of Evolution. Ever since Charles Darwin propounded it, this theory has unfortunately been a rallying point on the one hand for those who want to bring discredit on the Bible and on the other hand for those who want to bring discredit on science.

At the outset, one misunderstanding must be corrected. Sometimes Christians will claim that the term 'theory' means that these ideas are far from being accepted by scientists at large. This is erroneous. As we said earlier, scientists use the terms 'theory' and 'law' almost interchangeably. A 'hypothesis' or 'conjecture' is something which still needs evidence to give it respectability. Not so a theory. Though in ordinary parlance we may say, 'Oh, but that's just a theory!', this is not the way scientists commonly use this term. The Quantum Theory or the Special Theory of Relativity, to name but two, are some of the best attested collections of laws to be found.

The case for evolution

There are currently millions of species of living things in the world. Have these all been separately created? The Theory of Evolution is, in a nutshell, that all living things have developed ('evolved') from a single original living form. Over millions of years all different species have been derived in this way.

Changes can be seen in living things. Mankind has bred dogs differing in kind from the Chihuahua to the St. Bernard. Bacteria develop immunity to certain antibiotics.

If one compares the skeletons of creatures with backbones (vertebrates), corresponding bones and structures are apparent. The flippers of whales and the wings of birds show the same bone structures which appear in the bones of our arms and hands, for instance. Sometimes apparently useless structures correspond to useful structures in other creatures. Some snakes, though possessing no limbs, nevertheless have bones which correspond to hips, for instance. Such structural evidence points to a common formation, and so possibly a common ancestry.

The fossil record adds the time dimension to the evidence. When fossil remains of animals are dated (such as by radioactivity), creatures appear to have developed as a tree of species. Some branches have become extinct (the dinosaurs being the best-known of these), whilst others appear to have moved through various changes towards species known today (of which the horse is a good example). Such a tree cannot be traced fully through the fossils, but although the detail may at times be incomplete, the pattern is evident.

In recent years genetics has added extra evidence. The nucleus of each cell contains long molecules of DNA (deoxyribonucleic acid). These comprise most of the information needed for building and running the organism. These molecules are divided into strings called chromosomes. Along the chromosomes are segments of information known as genes. Each gene is responsible for certain activities, such as the manufacture of particular proteins.

It has been found that the closer one would assign creatures on the tree of evolution, the greater the number of genes which they have in common. However, particular genes may be common to a large number of species, so that a bacterium and man share many genes which perform the same function in both. Once again, a common formation is indicated, which may be taken as evidence of a common ancestry.

Because of evidence such as this, it is now almost universally accepted by scientists working in this area that all species evolved from a single common ancestor.

Objections to evolution
Why is it that the Theory of Evolution has had such a bad press from many evangelical Christians? There are several reasons for this.

If evolution has indeed happened, then one consequence must be that the earth is many millions of years old. The processes of evolution do not happen overnight. Christians who believe that Genesis 1 may only be interpreted literally (as a creation in seven days of 24 hours) cannot accept that the universe is so old. Therefore the evolutionary theory is seen as opposing Biblical doctrine. As we have seen above, cosmology gives us evidence for a universe which is billions of years old. Perhaps this would have given adequate time for evolution.

The Theory of Evolution has no adequate explanation for the fact that man is so different from all other creatures. This might be considered a matter of man being simply 'more than' the animals. Some animals are intelligent, but man is more so. Some animals use sound signals, but man's use of language is more complex. However, many people would not be satisfied with an explanation merely based on matters of scale and degree. In some areas man is fundamentally different. Man has a moral sense. As Mark Twain said, 'Man is the Only Animal that Blushes. Or needs to.' Man may also display an appreciation of God; the faculty which Christians would term the soul or spirit. Man is not just an animal 'only more so'. He is an animal but not just an animal. If evolution happened, then it seems that God did an extra work of creation in enduing two primate individuals with souls.

One other aspect of evolution is unacceptable to most Christians. This is the idea that man is on an evolutionary journey which will make successive generations better and better. This concept was popular in the early twentieth century, but two world wars have served to dent it. It should be pointed out that this is a sociological idea which does not necessarily form part of the scientific Theory of Evolution. Sociologists have also tried to use the Theory of Relativity to show that moral values are relative, but this is false science, not truly science at all.

Because of the repugnance which some Christians have developed towards the Theory of Evolution, there have been many attempts to discredit it which are hardly fair. Attempts have been made to squeeze all the discovered history of the universe into several thousand years, even supposing in certain instances that the speed of light has varied enormously. Attention has been focused on the inaccuracies of dating by means of radioactivity, but there has usually been a failure to point out that such inaccuracies cannot be used to bring the timescale anywhere near the desired thousands of years. The small amount of anomalous fossil evidence has been given exaggerated prominence without regard to the huge and growing bulk of evidence for the evolutionary theory.

It has even been said that this is 'an ungodly theory'. I do not know what this can mean, unless people are contending that it goes against the inflexible interpretations of the Bible which they hold, and therefore must be ungodly. But what if God chose to use this method to create the species? We would then by our interpretation be asserting that the method God used in his work was an ungodly method, which is surely blasphemous.

The Bible and evolution

It is not impossible to harmonise the Bible account of creation and the Theory of Evolution. In doing so, it is necessary to realise that the Bible is not intended to be a manual of science. Its purpose is to bring God's message to mankind. What profit would it have been to the ancient Israelites to have been given a detailed description of the origin of species?

What we can expect, however, is that the two accounts, that of the Bible and that of science, should not be incompatible. For that to be the case, both the Bible and science have to be sympathetically interpreted.

Genesis chapter 1 contains a description of the emergence of different forms of life which is remarkably in agreement with the Theory of Evolution. Plant life appeared first (vv. 11–12). Animal life in the water (vv. 20–2) preceded animal life on land (vv. 24–5). Man was the latecomer on the scene (vv. 26–7). The only major disparity is that of 'birds' appearing before animal life on land (vv. 20–2), but this is not an insuperable obstacle if one interprets this as 'flying things', i.e. flying insects.

From the Bible we find that man is different from the beasts, as we noted above. When God formed man, he made him from 'the dust of the ground' and 'breathed into his nostrils the breath of life' (Genesis 2:7). Man's body is not specially distinguished from that of all other animals, but his spirit is.

This description does not rule out the possibility that man's body was in line of descent from the bodies of the creatures which had preceded him, but that God performed a special act of creation for man's spirit. This view is encouraged by the Hebrew of Genesis chapter 1. The word 'create' (Heb. *bara*) is used only in verses 1, 21 and 27. Elsewhere the word used is *'asah* 'make'. This distinction is preserved in the New International Version. If we are right in seeing a distinction between these words, they would indicate a special intervention by God in the case of the first animals and in the case of man.

In all of this, it is only possible to harmonise the words of scripture with the findings of science if we interpret the 'days' of Genesis chapter 1 figuratively. Cosmology also requires this. This for some Christians is the sticking point. However, it must be pointed out that the clash then between the Bible and science lies not in what the Bible says, but in how strongly we cling to one particular interpretation.

Intelligent Design

In recent years there has been another attack on the Theory of Evolution by Christians who are also scientists. They have pointed out that evolution can only conceivably operate if at every stage of development what was produced could operate usefully. A complicated structure could not have originated by natural selection in one jump. It must have evolved by a series of small changes.

It has been pointed out that the flagellum (a whip-like whisker) by means of which some bacteria move around is a very complex structure. It is hard to imagine that it could come about by means of small incremental changes. Therefore, say these scientists, this is evidence of an intelligent designer (God?) who made the change.

It should be pointed out that Creationism and Intelligent Design are poles apart. The creationists, intent on interpreting the Bible literally, deny a great deal of the evidence which scientists have discovered about the universe. The proponents of Intelligent Design, on the other hand, accept the scientific evidence, and agree that evolution explains much of what has happened in the origin and development of different species. They would simply focus on those areas where the Theory of Evolution has difficulty, and would say that these areas constitute evidence for a supernatural designer.

Those who have read about the clash between science and Christianity in the last century may here feel a sense of *deja vu*. In the early twentieth century there were attempts to see God's hand in the universe. These were known as 'the God of the gaps'. If you see that scientists have difficulty in explaining anything, then postulate that God must have done it. Unfortunately, when scientists do manage to discover a material explanation for the phenomenon, then 'the God of the gaps' is diminished in scope.

If someone really did demonstrate that the material universe gives evidence of a supernatural designer, then he or she would probably win a Nobel prize. But such a demonstration needs to provide positive evidence, not just the negative assertion that scientists have not yet discovered an adequate explanation.

Conclusions

When the findings of science are harmonised with the words of scripture, an astonishing fact stands out. It is not the case that the Bible and science are at loggerheads. It is not even the case that they each address their own area and do not impinge on one another. It is that the Bible and science in part travel the same road together.

The concept of the Big Bang tallies with the Bible: God at a particular instant created the heavens and the earth. The order of appearance of living things in Genesis 1 corresponds very well with the geological record.

The desire of some Christians to cling to an interpretation of the Bible which is as literal as possible has led to an unedifying situation. Attacks are made on what is seen as weak points in the scientists' arguments. This in itself is perfectly valid, and is done by other scientists as part of their work. However, scientists seek to replace what is deficient by another theory which covers all the evidence. I have not seen any such thorough-going alternative theory advanced by those who dispute science on the basis of the

Bible. A guerilla fighter seeks to snipe at particular vulnerable points, but his aim is simply destruction, not the rebuilding of society. Some Christians seem to snipe at science in a similar vein.

Sadly, some Christians seem ready even to find solace in conspiracy theories, accusing non-Christian scientists of deliberately distorting the evidence so as to force conflicts with the scriptures. This idea ignores the fact that the basis of science is to let the evidence dictate the shape of the theory, not to ram the foot into a shoe of the wrong shape. It also ignores the fact that many scientists are themselves Bible-believing Christians.

Science should not contradict the Bible. After all, scientists are simply investigating the universe which was made by the God who authored the Bible. Though God may overrule the laws of nature in order to work a miracle, normally those laws are in effect. Science may well contradict our *interpretation* of the Bible, however.

Maybe some Christians have deeper problems. It is not just that they are antagonistic to scientists, suspecting them of a plot against Christianity. It is not just that they have an aversion to scientific theories, suspecting them of contradicting the Bible. It is perhaps that they have a quarrel with science itself. Investigating the way the world works seems to them an invalid pursuit, because it may produce ideas which run counter to their literalistic view of the Bible. This is why they seek to oppose theories which are trying to explain the data in a reasonable way.

We have two choices before us. We can persist in our interpretation, and insist that it is the universe which gives the wrong impression to our senses. Or we can, as suggested in Chapter 2, 'Consider the context of the world around us' when we investigate how to interpret the Bible.

Which seems the better way to you?

11

The last things

'The Welsh like the gospel because it gives them something to sing about; the Irish like the gospel because it gives them something to fight about; and the Scots like the gospel because it is free.' So goes the adage.

One part of the gospel which seems to be fought over more than any other is the doctrine of 'the last things', called by the theologians 'eschatology' (which means just about the same thing, but is Greek).

What will happen when God winds up the universe? Theories and schemes abound, and each one has its advocates. Sometimes it seems that the less scriptural evidence there is for an idea, the more firmly it is clung to, and the more animosity is reserved for those who seek to differ.

How can we dare to open such a can of worms? I will not be able to consider the great number of theories which have been proposed. However, my aim in this book is not to deal with many schemes, but rather to show how any scheme may be examined in the light of the principles presented in Chapter 2 and the Biblical themes in Chapters 3 to 6. These tools will serve to show which schemes are more likely to be right, and which are most suspect.

In this chapter I will seek to home in on only one such scheme, but it is one which has achieved considerable popularity and which has influenced many people who perhaps would not recognise this scheme in its entirety.

The millennium

One matter which is at the heart of many theories of the last things is that of the millennium, so you will need to understand what this about.

A millennium is 1000 years. The millennium in question is only mentioned specifically in Revelation 20:1-3:

And I saw an angel coming down out of heaven, having the key to the Abyss and holding in his hand a great chain. He seized the dragon, that ancient serpent, who is the devil, or Satan, and bound him for a thousand years. He threw him into the Abyss, and locked and sealed it over him, to keep him from deceiving the nations any more until the thousand years were ended. After that, he must be set free for a short time.

This 1000 years is described as the time during which those who have been executed (the Greek word means 'killed with an axe') because of their witness to Christ will come to life and reign.

Let us consider this in the light of the principles proposed in Chapter 2. Revelation is far from being a clear book to interpret, and this passage is perhaps the most difficult part of the book. There are three main interpretations which have been advanced which differ according to when Christ is going to take the church to himself. These three are known as 'premillennial', 'postmillennial' and 'amillennial'.

Premillennial
This interpretation supposes that Christ will take the church to heaven before ('pre-') the 1000 years. Messiah will then reign over the earth for this period, during which time the devil will be prevented from hindering.

Postmillennial
This sees the 1000 years being a time of blessing for the church at the end of this current age. Christ will return for the church after ('post-') the millennium.

Amillennial
The millennium is seen not ('a-') as a literal 1000 years, but as symbolic of all the time between Christ's life on earth and the second coming. The devil's activity is seen as restricted because of Christ's triumphant death and resurrection.

There are difficulties in all three of these positions. The passage speaks of martyrs, not of the church as a whole. Their reign could be in heaven rather than on earth. In terms of the principles of Chapter 2, we find it difficult to start with what is clear, because it is hard to find any clear passage from which to start.

The story is told of a man who saw that the minister, on leaving the church, had dropped his sermon notes. When he picked them up, he saw that one part read, 'Argument weak here: shout louder!'

At this point you should hear the alarm bells ringing. An obscure passage is the only one to mention the millennium, yet this concept is made central to many theories about the last things. Some believers will then contend vigorously for the theories they espouse. We are on very dangerous ground.

Of these three positions, the premillennial view foretells a time after Christ has come for the church when much will happen on the earth. This theory in particular requires a number of questions to be answered. Will it still be possible then for people to believe in Christ and be saved through grace? How will God deal with people in that age? These are questions which have been addressed by some in terms of 'dispensations'.

The dispensations

The most common form of premillennialism is a system called 'dispensationalism'. (I apologise for the awful terminology. Stick with it!) Perhaps you are thinking to yourself, 'What on earth have I to do with dispensations, whatever they are?' Perhaps they have more relevance to you than you realise.

The system of dispensationalism has spread far and wide, and reached to those who may never have heard of the term. It has been particularly influential in shaping how many Christians regard the second coming of Christ, the millennium, the Jews and the land of Israel. The concepts were circulated largely through the *Scofield Reference Bible* (copyright 1917, Oxford University Press). A Bible with notes throughout, to tell you, when you read any passage, how to interpret that passage, is a powerful tool. Unfortunately, it can also hinder the process of letting the Bible speak for itself, and can bias a fair assessment of true interpretation. So we need our principles and themes to weigh up its findings.

Scofield asserts that there are seven 'dispensations' in the Bible. By these, he apparently means seven periods of history marked by different relationships between God and mankind. His dispensations, with the periods assigned to them, are as follows:

1. Innocency. Adam and Eve in the garden before the fall.
2. Conscience. From the fall to the flood.
3. Human government. After the flood up to the tower of Babel.
4. Promise. From God's call of Abraham to the exodus from Egypt.
5. Law. From the giving of the law up to the crucifixion.
6. Grace. From the crucifixion up to Christ coming again for the church.
7. Kingdom. God's dealings with Israel after the church is taken.

When you read Scofield, the periods of these seven dispensations are clear. If you do not have the benefit of Scofield's notes, though, it is not obvious that this is the way the Bible must be interpreted. The foundation for these ideas does not seem to be either broad or deep. You need to ask yourself, would they pass the desert island test of Chapter 2?

Note that it is only during dispensation number 6 that Scofield sees God dealing with men by means of the gospel of his grace. This is the church period. The period when Christ was teaching here on earth was still part of the dispensation of law, and during that time the gospel of the kingdom was preached for Israel, says Scofield. At the end of the church period the church will be taken to be with Christ but the rest of humanity will remain on earth. This is the 'secret rapture', where 'rapture' is used in the sense of 'taking away'. After the church has gone, God will once again deal with his ancient people Israel.

We must now consider the ideas which are basic to dispensationalism, and see how they compare with the clearest words we can find in the scriptures.

The interlude of grace
Strict adherents to the dispensational system consider that virtually all of Christ's teaching when he was here on earth was for the sake of the kingdom of Israel, and not for the church. Some even go as far as to say that 'there is no gospel in the Gospels'. There is the gospel of the kingdom, they will say, but this is not the same as the gospel of the grace of God. Whilst perhaps not all would be so extreme, the term 'kingdom of God' in the gospels is supposed to refer to God's kingship over the Jews, not to the church.

The kingdom is seen as the Messianic rule of Christ the Son of David, and so is reserved for the relationship between Christ and the Jews. It is not considered to be applicable to the church. This 'kingdom of God' was in effect throughout the dispensation of law (until the crucifixion) and then is suspended during the dispensation of grace. When Christ comes and takes the church to himself, this 'kingdom' is then applicable once more.

In fact, some see the church period, the dispensation of grace, as an interlude. All God's prophecies in the Old Testament are put on hold while the church is born, while it proclaims the gospel of grace, and then is taken to be with Christ. Some have said that during this interval 'the prophetic clock stops ticking.'

Is there really such a difference between the gospel which Christ preached on earth and that preached after his death? In the gospels Jesus proclaimed good news based on his sacrificial death for us (Mark 10:45). He told Nicodemus that unless he was born again he could not see the kingdom of God (John 3:3). Everyone who believes in Christ has eternal life, we are told (John 3:16). What is this but the gospel of the grace of God?

During the church period Philip in Samaria preached 'the good news of the kingdom of God and the name of Jesus Christ' and men and women were baptized (Acts 8:12). Paul and Barnabas told the disciples that 'we must go through many hardships to enter the kingdom of God' (Acts 14:22). Paul lived in Rome and 'preached the kingdom of God and taught about the Lord Jesus Christ' (Acts 28:31). In all of these cases the preaching was to Gentiles. Paul declares that 'the kingdom of God' is 'righteousness, peace and joy in the Holy Spirit' (Romans 14:17). Were these people, when they spoke of the kingdom, not speaking about the gospel of the grace of God?

It appears that there is only one gospel. There is only one way to be saved. This is clearly made known in Hebrews: 'How shall we escape if we ignore such a great salvation? This salvation, which was first announced by the Lord, was confirmed to us by those who heard him' (Hebrews 2:3). The writer to the Hebrews is saying that Jesus (the Lord) declared this salvation. Those who heard him (the apostles) also bore witness to this same message. This is the message which we are exhorted not to neglect in this, the church period. What Jesus preached and what the apostles preached was the same. It was the same gospel all along. This tallies with the theme we saw in Chapter 3. There is now only one way of salvation, only one gospel, the gospel of the grace of God through Christ's sacrifice on the cross.

The conclusion one comes to is that the gospel of the kingdom of God is identical with the gospel of the grace of God, the gospel which was preached by the early church.

The second coming

The premillennial view requires two returns for Christ. One is the time when he will come to take his people to himself. The second is when he comes after the millennium to execute judgement on all people.

There are three Greek words used to refer to Christ's coming. These are *parousia* ('coming'), *epiphaneia* ('appearing') and *apokalypsis* ('revelation'). Attempts have been made to allocate these words to different comings, but with little success. Believers are encouraged to wait for Christ's *parousia* (James 5:7), for his *epiphaneia* (Titus 2:13) and for his *apokalypsis* (1 Corinthians 1:7).

The New Testament speaks of God giving his people relief at the same time as he comes in judgement on the ungodly. This seems to be most clearly expressed in 2 Thessalonians 1:6–8:

> *God is just: He will pay back trouble to those who trouble you and give relief to you who are troubled, and to us as well. This will happen when the Lord Jesus is revealed from heaven in blazing fire with his powerful angels. He will punish those who do not know God and do not obey the gospel of our Lord Jesus.*

These verses make plain that at one and the same time (a) God will grant rest to his people; (b) the Lord Jesus will be revealed in his glorious second coming; (c) unbelievers and persecutors of the church will suffer his final judgement, 'eternal destruction and shut out from the presence of the Lord' (v. 9).

Christ spoke about the coming of the Son of man, when two people will be together, and one will be taken and one left (Matthew 24:40, 41). The context of Matthew chapter 24 is (vv. 30–1):

They will see the Son of Man coming on the clouds of the sky, with power and great glory. And he will send his angels with a loud trumpet call, and they will gather his elect from the four winds, from one end of the heavens to the other.

This can hardly be described as secret. The whole world will know. Revelation 1:7 also describes Christ 'coming with the clouds', and adds, 'every eye will see him'. Can you find clear evidence in the Bible for a secret coming of Christ for his church and a subsequent, much later, glorious coming to bring an end to this present age? I must confess that I cannot.

It seems clear that when Christ comes again for his people, it will be in glory, and will signal the end of history.

After the church

What happens after the church is taken to be with Christ? The dispensationalist sees this as a different dispensation, when the world goes through the great tribulation and then during the millennium the Messianic kingdom of Christ is established with the nation of Israel.

According to dispensationalists, it is during this period that God once again takes up his ancient people Israel, the Jews, and deals with them according to the Law. The Messianic kingdom is established. Some even consider that at that time the temple will be rebuilt and animal sacrifices offered once again. The re-establishment of the nation of Israel in recent times is seen as a foreshadowing of God dealing in these ways.

In Chapters 3 to 6 we traced some of the major themes of the New Testament, and likened these to the framework which gives strength to a skyscraper. These themes are so fundamental and so clearly displayed in the scriptures that any other themes which are being suggested must be judged by them.

We saw that Christ's sacrifice provided a way of salvation which is once for all God's unique way of restoring people to fellowship with himself. We saw that God's people, his new Israel, comprises all who trust in Christ for salvation, whether they are physically descended from Israel or not. We saw that the promised land is interpreted in the New Testament in spiritual terms as the place where God is to be found. We saw that Christ abolished the Law by fulfilling it.

Premilliennial theories expect that there will be a period after the church is gone when God deals with people in a way different from his dealings in the present church age. Usually it is expected that God once again will take up the Jews simply because of their physical descent and irrespective of their faith in Christ. In some way they are to be saved, even if it is not by trusting in the salvation which is the keystone of the church period. God is expected to return to dealing with people on the basis of the Law even though in the Old Testament (Jeremiah 31:31ff) he promised that he was inaugurating a better covenant. As for restarting the temple sacrifices, these fly in the face of Christ's sacrifice, once for all, ending all other sacrifices.

Not only are these ideas founded on unclear passages (and very few of them), but they contradict the main themes which we saw to be securely established.

What does it matter?
It is a shame that the subject of the last things has become a happy hunting ground for those with ideas which have little or no secure foundation in the scriptures. There are passages in the New Testament about this subject which are not only clear but also of great relevance to us in our daily lives.

As someone said, 'It isn't the passages I don't understand that worry me; it's those I do understand!'

We know for sure that Christ is going to return to take those of us who believe in him to be with him (John 14:3). We can take comfort in the fact that believers who have died will also join with us, to be with the Lord for ever (1 Thessalonians 4:13-18).

The fact that the end of the universe as we know it is imminent brings a moral responsibility on us to live holy and godly lives (2 Peter 3:10-13). We must be ready for Christ to come at an unexpected time, fulfilling the responsibilities he has given us towards the rest of his servants (Matthew 24:42-51).

In preparing for the coming of Christ we will hardly have time to bother ourselves with outlandish ideas which have little foundation in the Bible as a whole. And a good thing too, if these ideas run counter to the major themes of Christ and his salvation.

12

Miracles

'The age of miracles is past', people say. The Bible is full of miracles, yet they are not often seen nowadays. Why is this so? Should it be so? We need to apply the principles suggested in Chapter 2, and look at the whole sweep of the subject. We have plenty of material to work on.

Supernatural happenings seen in public are referred to in the New Testament as 'signs and wonders'. Signs and wonders are not necessarily two classes of events. A 'sign' is a supernatural event which carries a message, pointing people to a particular fact. A 'wonder' is something which causes people to wonder, to marvel, to be amazed. Together they comprise what we would call 'miracles'.

A miracle is something which cuts across the laws of the natural world. When someone believes in Christ and becomes a new creation, that in itself is a miracle. People also speak poetically of the miracle of spring, of new lambs, of opening flowers and suchlike. However, in this chapter the miracles about which I am writing are times when God intervenes in ways which the laws of science would not anticipate and cannot explain.

Before considering whether the age of miracles is indeed past, we need to consider what kinds of miracles were performed in the New Testament, and what their purpose was.

Jesus' miracles

When you read the New Testament, you cannot fail to be struck by the number of supernatural happenings described there.

Jesus' life was filled with miracles. He healed people from all kinds of illnesses. The pages of the gospels are full of instances. In particular, he healed diseases which were considered incurable. He healed lepers (who may not have been suffering from Hansen's Disease, but were certainly considered incurable) (Matthew 8:2-4; Mark 1:40-4; Luke 5:12-14; 17:11-19). He healed a woman who had haemorrhaged for 12 years and who could not be healed by the doctors (Mark 5:25-34; Luke 8:43-8). He raised the dead back to life again, notably the widow of Nain's son (Luke 7:11-16), Jairus' daughter (Matt. 9:23-5; Mark 5:38-43; Luke 8:49-56) and Lazarus (John 11:43-4; 12:1, 9, 17). Many times over it is recorded that Jesus cast out evil spirits from people.

Apart from healing disease, Jesus asserted his authority over the natural world in stilling the storm (Matt. 8:24-6; Mark 4:37-41; Luke 8:23-5). Jesus cursed the fig tree and it withered (Matt. 21:19; Mark 11:13-14, 20-1).

The greatest miracle which Jesus performed is that he rose from the dead. A man told his friend that he had had a great idea for a new religion. How should he promote it? His friend told him, 'Preach it far and wide, and when people get annoyed with you, get them to kill you. Then after three days, rise again from the dead!'

The disciples' miracles

Jesus gave the 12 disciples authority 'to drive out evil spirits and to heal every disease and sickness' (Matthew 10:1). He instructed them to 'heal the sick, raise the dead, cleanse those who have leprosy, drive out demons' (v. 8). This did not just apply to the apostles. The 70 (72?) who were sent out were also told to 'heal the sick' (Luke 10:9). Jesus told them, 'I have given you authority . . . to overcome all the power of the enemy' (Luke 10:19).

Miracles did not stop happening when Christ ascended. As someone has said, the 'Acts of the Apostles' should be renamed the 'Acts of the Holy Spirit', because many works of power were accomplished by the Spirit working through God's people.

The gift of speaking in languages you have not learned, so that native speakers of those languages can understand (Acts 2:7-11) was the first of these miracles. Then there was the healing of the man crippled from birth sitting at the temple gate (Acts 3:1-10). 'The apostles performed many miraculous signs and wonders' (Acts 5:12). These included many healings. 'All were healed' (v. 16) we are told. Paul in Malta prayed and laid his hands on Publius' father and saw him healed (Acts 28:7-8), with the consequence that 'the rest of the sick on the island came and were cured' (v. 9).

The dead were raised to life through the apostles, as we see with Peter in the case of Tabitha (Acts 9:36-42). This was also true for Paul when Eutychus fell out of the window when Paul 'talked on and on' (Acts 20:9). The young man was 'picked up dead' (v. 9), but when Paul put his arms around him he came to life (vv. 10-12).

Paul declared that he had 'fully proclaimed the gospel of Christ' (Romans 15:19) 'by the power of signs and miracles, through the power of the Spirit'. He said his preaching was accompanied by 'a demonstration of the Spirit's power' (1 Corinthians 2:4).

Not all miracles were positive in their effect. At Paphos Paul cursed the false prophet Bar-Jesus and brought blindness on him (Acts 13:9-12).

The gifts of the Spirit listed in 1 Corinthians 12 are all of miraculous origin. They include the word of wisdom, the word of knowledge, gifts of healing, miraculous powers, prophecy, distinguishing between spirits, speaking in tongues and the interpretation of tongues.

Hearing God speak to you personally is also something which is supernatural. This happened, for instance, to Philip. An angel of the Lord told him to go south to the road from Jerusalem to Gaza (Acts 8:26), so that he could meet up with the Ethiopian eunuch. We do not know whether Philip heard an actual voice, or whether the message came through a strong impression in his mind. Such messages occurred often (Acts 9:10-16; 10:3-6, 13-15, 19-20; 13:2 etc.) Hearing from God is also, of course, a necessary prerequisite for prophesying.

The reasons for miracles
If the New Testament is so full of miracles, we need to ask why. What was the reason behind all these works of power? These things did not happen just by chance. How did they fit into God's purpose of redemption? Several reasons may readily be discerned for them.

Alleviation
Many times in the gospels we are given the reason for Jesus healing the sick. He was concerned for the suffering of the people. He had compassion for the leper (Mark 1:41), for the widow of Nain (Luke 7:13), for the blind men (Matt. 20:34).

Jesus saw the woman who could not straighten as being kept bound by Satan, and needing to be set free (Luke 13:16). Peter declared that Jesus of Nazareth 'went about doing good and healing all who were under the power of the devil' (Acts 10:38). 'The reason the Son of God appeared was to destroy the devil's work' (1 John 3:8).

Accreditation
One of the major reasons for miracles is that God, through these supernatural happenings, set his seal on people. On the day of Pentecost Peter describes Jesus in these words: 'Jesus of Nazareth was a man accredited by God to you by miracles, wonders and signs, which God did among you through him' (Acts 2:22). When John the Baptist in prison sends to enquire whether Jesus is really the Christ, Jesus points him to the evidence: 'The blind receive sight, the lame walk, those who have leprosy are cured, the deaf hear, the dead are raised, and the good news is preached to the poor' (Matthew 11:5). The greatest accreditation is given by the

greatest of miracles. Christ was 'declared with power to be the Son of God by his resurrection from the dead' (Romans 1:4).

Apostles are also accredited by the miracles which God performs at their hands. Paul refers to 'the things that mark an apostle—signs, wonders and miracles' (2 Corinthians 12:12).

Affirmation
As the gospel is proclaimed, God affirms that it is true by causing miracles to accompany the preaching. 'This salvation, which was first announced by the Lord, was confirmed to us by those who heard him. God also testified to it by signs, wonders and various miracles, and gifts of the Holy Spirit distributed according to his will' (Hebrews 2:3-4).

This theme appears a number of times in the New Testament. The Lord 'confirmed his word by the signs and wonders that accompanied it' (Mark 16:20). God 'confirmed the message of his grace by enabling them to do miraculous signs and wonders' (Acts 14:3).

Revealing God
Jesus' compassion for the needy shows us something of God's heart as he healed those who were suffering. Jesus himself declared the purpose behind healing the man blind from birth as being 'that the work of God might be displayed' (John 9:3). The raising of Lazarus was, he said, 'for the glory of God' (John 11:4).

When the disciples were sent out to preach and heal the heart of their message was to be 'The kingdom of heaven is near' (Matthew 10:7).

Spiritual gifts are used by God to build up both individual believers and the church as a whole (1 Corinthians 14:4).

The miracles performed in the New Testament were to show that God is both compassionate and powerful, healing the suffering and demonstrating that he has come to reign.

The promise of miracles
Paul refers to God as 'he who gives you the Spirit and works miracles among you' (Galatians 3:5, Greek). This is how we are to regard God. Jesus certainly expected that miracle-working would continue, and would even increase (John 14:12):

Anyone who has faith in me will do what I have been doing. He will even do greater things than these, because I am going to the Father.

The end of Mark's gospel, much discussed and yet still included within the scriptures, declares that signs and wonders will accompany those who believe (Mark 16:17-18). Paul exhorts his readers to 'eagerly desire spiritual gifts, especially the gift of prophecy' (1 Corinthians 14:1). He adds, 'I would like every one of you to speak in tongues, but I would rather have you prophesy' (v. 5). 'Be eager to prophesy, and do not forbid speaking in tongues' (v. 39).

It is obvious that in New Testament times the miraculous was an integral part of the spread of the gospel and the life of the Christian.

Have they gone?
The church has historically not seen much of the supernatural. How can we explain this? In the New Testament miraculous operations were part and parcel of God's activity. This is in stark contrast to much of the church today. Church services and coffee mornings abound. People experience the miracle of new birth. God also speaks to believers to guide them. But generally signs and wonders are unknown.

Because of this state of affairs, non-Christians and modernists have expressed doubts as to whether the miracles really took place in the first century. This cynicism is expressed by a character in George Gershwin's folk opera *Porgy and Bess*:

It ain't necessarily so.
Dem tings dat you're li'ble to read in de Bible,
It ain't necessarily so.

Two possible explanations suggest themselves. One is that the church has lacked faith and the power of the Holy Spirit. The other is that God no longer chooses to work by means of the supernatural.

No one finds it comfortable to admit that they have been deficient in any way, and that they continue to be deficient. If the church has indeed lacked the power of the Holy Spirit, then the consequence is that one needs to ask how this may be restored. An easier option is to suppose that God has his own reasons for removing the supernatural from the church.

A book I was reading by a keen evangelical pointed out that there had been almost no miracles in the last few centuries. The writer gave this fact as evidence that miracles were no longer to be expected. God did not work miracles in our midst any more. If you suggested to this man that Christianity was to be determined by tradition, he would be horrified, I am sure. Yet the tradition of 'no miracles' is a fact of life for him.

The sovereignty of God

One possible reason which has been suggested for the absence of miracles nowadays is the sovereignty of God. He 'works out everything in conformity with the purpose of his will' (Ephesians 1:11). Perhaps his will during the last few hundred years has been not to perform miracles.

Undeniably we see God's sovereignty in particular instances. God will not perform miracles simply because we want him to do so. We pray for healing, and sometimes we do not see it happen. Paul left Trophimus ill in Miletus (2 Timothy 4:21). We cry to God for him to come in and change situations, but he does not always respond as we would like. God is sovereign in such matters.

God is also sovereign in the way he dispenses his gifts. Hebrews speaks of 'gifts of the Holy Spirit distributed according to his will' (Hebrews 2:4). God shares out spiritual gifts, giving them 'to each one, just as he determines' (1 Corinthians 12:11).

However, there is surely a difference between what happens in particular cases and the way God works in general. After informing us through the scriptures that miracles are his way of endorsing his gospel and his servants, would God in his sovereignty change his whole method of working? After distributing spiritual gifts for building up individuals and the church, would he cause them suddenly to dry up completely? More than that, would he do so without giving notice of these things through the Bible? This hardly seems to be what we would expect, since 'the Sovereign Lord does nothing without revealing his plan to his servants the prophets' (Amos 3:7).

We cannot explain all deficiencies in the visible church in terms of the sovereignty of God alone. Was it due to God's sovereignty that the gospel of grace all but disappeared before the Reformation? This was surely due to man's deficiency, not to God's intent. The absence of miracles in many parts of the church for such a long period of time may similarly show that Christians have been out of step with God's intentions for his church, and therefore have failed to pray for miracles and to expect them.

The complete Bible

Those who consider that miracles are not for today usually suppose that signs and wonders are no longer needed. In the age before the scriptures were complete, they would say, people needed supernatural evidences. However, now we have the whole Bible, this revelation takes the place of these signs.

Such people obviously believe that there has been a phase change, like that between ice and water, or like that between the Old Testament and the New. The working of miracles has now been replaced by the provision of the whole Bible. If there were such a radical phase change, should we not be told? This idea certainly seeks to exalt the scriptures, making them more important than the working of God with power through great miracles. If the scriptures are indeed so great, we would surely expect that in them we would find a clear indication that a phase change is to be anticipated.

We are hard put to it to find scriptures which give any indication that miracles were only to be temporary. There is only one passage which seems to come near, and that is 1 Corinthians 13:8: 'Where there are prophecies, they will cease; where there are tongues, they will be stilled; where there is knowledge, it will pass away.' The chapter shows that love is vital, and the exercise of spiritual gifts without love is worthless. Prophecies and speaking in tongues (two of the spiritual gifts) will come to an end. It is hard to see that knowledge as such will ever end, so perhaps Paul is referring here to another of the gifts of the Spirit, the word of knowledge. But when will these gifts end? Does this refer to the completion of the canon of scripture, when all the New Testament is complete, or does it speak of a future age when we are for ever with the Lord?

If this passage in 1 Corinthians 13 is to prepare the church for the cessation of miracles (and spiritual gifts with them) when the scripture is complete, it is astonishing that no mention is made here of the scriptures. For a teaching to be established from the Bible we expect to find clear scriptures on the subject, and we expect sufficient evidence. Do you think there is enough evidence to convince you of such a significant change in God's working?

Do we need them?

In the story of Aladdin the wicked magician roams the streets offering 'New lamps for old!' Those who heard him should have smelled a rat, because it was not a fair exchange. We need to consider whether swapping miracles for the full Bible would be a fair exchange.

As far as the **alleviation** of illness, we do now have modern medicine and, in Britain, a National Health Service. Perhaps we are not so much in need of God's miraculous activity in healing. However, there are illnesses for which medicine has not yet found a cure. There are sometimes long waiting lists. Sometimes the most important healing is not of body, but of the heart and mind. People are racked by hurts of the past. Moreover, if it is the case that our enemy the devil sends his minions into people's lives to harry them, then we still need to bring God's power to bear in casting out those evil spirits. We cannot expect such deliverance from the National Health Service. God still wants to show his love and concern for individuals in need. It hardly seems that God would stop healing people simply because he has given them the whole of the Bible.

If miracles were necessary for the **accreditation** of Christian leaders, then it is hard to see how the scriptures can perform the same task. Can a man be approved merely because he has a Bible in his hand? Even those who appear to live lives true to the scriptures may have skeletons in their private cupboards.

God gave **affirmation** of his word, confirming the good news by accompanying signs and thereby showing that this message was true. How can the scriptures fulfil this need? Is the message of the scriptures sufficient to confirm the message of the scriptures? What God promises in his word is miraculous, so signs and wonders give affirmation not just of the spoken word but also confirmation of what is written.

The scriptures are certainly effective in **revealing God**. They show that God is loving and caring, able to help those in need. One way in which he does this is by the alleviation of illness, for example. So the scriptures point the way, but the miracles are surely the fulfilment of what the scriptures teach.

Jesus' condemnation of the Sadducees was that they knew neither the scriptures nor the power of God (Matthew 22:29). Both are surely needed. If a Formula 1 racing driver heard that you had removed his accelerator pedal, would he be reassured to know that you had at least left him the service manual?

False miracles
We need to face the fact here that miracles are not necessarily the result of God's power. The enemy, the devil, can also work wonders. Jesus spoke of false Christs and false prophets arising to 'perform great signs and miracles' (Matthew 24:24). Paul warned his readers of 'the work of Satan displayed in all kinds of counterfeit miracles, signs and wonders' (2 Thessalonians 2:9). Those who never knew Christ will point to the 'many miracles' which they did in his name (Matt. 7:22).

Besides these miracles worked by the enemy, those Christians who believe in miracles may be unwise in their methods. They may pray for healing, and then reassure the sick person that they have been healed even though the symptoms remain. If healing does not happen, they may condemn the sufferer for his sin, or for lack of faith. In ways like this they may not be able to heal the sickness, but can leave the sick one in greater need pastorally than when they started.

The fact that a counterfeit exists, or that people may be unwise in their dealings, does not mean that the real thing does not exist. Fake antiques would not be snapped up so eagerly by the unwary if it were not for the fact that real antiques exist which are valuable.

How may we distinguish between miracles performed through the power of the Holy Spirit and those resulting from a very different spirit? One of the gifts of the Spirit is that of 'distinguishing between spirits' (1 Corinthians 12:10). Ironically, those who assert that the gifts of the Spirit have ceased and are not for us today, stand in particular need of this gift, which they claim has disappeared!

John gives us help in being able to 'test the spirits' (1 John 4:1). The key is that 'Every spirit that acknowledges that Jesus Christ has come in the flesh is from God' (v. 2). Do the miracles bring praise to the Lord Jesus Christ? Are they in conformity with all that we read in the scriptures about him and his working? Is their effect to reveal more of the nature of God to people?

Prove all things
There is one matter here which deserves the gravest of warnings. The Pharisees attempted to test the spirits where Christ was concerned, and concluded that his miracles were achieved by means of 'Beelzebub, the prince of demons' (Matthew 12:24). They considered the activity of the Holy Spirit operating through Christ and concluded that the power at work was that of the devil himself. Sadly, there have been evangelical believers who have been completely convinced that a phase change has taken place and that the gifts of the Spirit are no longer for today. When they have heard of such gifts being manifested they have concluded that this cannot be the work of the Holy Spirit and therefore it must be the work of the devil. Christ tells his hearers that speaking against himself is something which may be forgiven. However, 'anyone who speaks against the Holy Spirit will not be forgiven, either in this age or in the age to come' (v. 32).

Lessons
The church has become accustomed to living without seeing much of God's power. Perhaps it has been the case that some Christians have been

characterised as 'having a form of godliness but denying its power' (2 Timothy 3:5). In this situation it is easy for a church with little power to invent a theology of powerlessness. Such a state of affairs is self-perpetuating. We do not see miracles, so we produce reasons why we should not expect miracles. We see the continued absence of miracles as confirming our reasons that there should be no miracles. And so it goes on.

What we are doing by this process is developing lack of faith. When faith was lacking, not even Jesus could do many miracles (Matthew 13:58).

It has been a great cause for rejoicing that in recent years there has been more experience of the Spirit at work in the church worldwide, bringing people to new birth, filling Christians with joy and delight, engendering love and zeal for Christ—and working miracles.

If we see from the scriptures that signs and wonders are to be expected, then this will motivate us to pray for such things to happen in our times. We will have faith that God intends to show his power in this day and age. True miracles are the work of the Holy Spirit. We cannot expect the sovereign God to demonstrate his miraculous power simply to suit us. But we can implore him to make us clean and usable, to fill us with the power of his Spirit, and to display his glorious power through us.

Those who expect God to work miracles will be able to pray like the disciples in Acts 4:24-31. They addressed God as 'Sovereign Lord' (v. 24), acknowledging the primacy of his will and intentions. They nevertheless prayed, 'Stretch out your hand to heal and perform miraculous signs and wonders through the name of your holy servant Jesus' (v. 30). May we not ask him to do the same today?

13

The church

Not far from where we live there is a farm with Guernsey cows. The milk from these animals is used to produce wonderful ice cream in dozens of flavours.

If anyone were to count up how many flavours the Christian church comes in, the result would be anything but wonderful. Jesus prayed for believers 'that all of them may be one' (John 17:21). Externally, they are far from being this. Someone parodied the hymn 'Onward Christian soldiers' to read:

We are not united,
Not one body, we.

It appears that different groups of Christians have added extra layers ('traditions') to their churches. The layers added by different denominations differ, so this causes them to be distanced from one another. I heard a clergyman denounce this situation. The Methodists should rejoin the Anglican church, he said, and then the pair of them should rejoin the Catholics, who were there before them. And the new churches ought never to have come into existence. What he is suggesting is not only that some should forsake their layers, but also that they should take back some layers (e.g. from the Catholic church) which they had sought to relinquish.

The ecumenical movement has long campaigned for such amalgamations. Of course, the Bible tells us very little directly about denominations or what to do about it once they have sprung up. Nevertheless, there is much in the Bible to show how the church used to function from its origination, before any extra layers were added. Perhaps we have been used to getting our information about the church from our own denominations or traditions. It would be instructive if we could get it straight from the Bible.

Form and function

In this chapter we will look at the way churches operated in early times, sweeping through the whole New Testament and gleaning what information we can from it.

One difficulty must be dealt with at the outset. When we are confronted with a new type of church, our natural tendency is to concentrate on the outward forms and appearances. What form of church government do they follow? Do they have an organ or guitars? What hymn book do they use? Do they follow a liturgy? Use candles? Incense? An overhead projector?

What is more important than the form of a church is the way it functions. How does it represent the body of Christ on earth? Are people brought into a loving relationship with God and with one another? Is there true worship in the Holy Spirit? Are believers built up on the scriptures? Is the church reaching out effectively to those round about?

No matter how hard you try, form cannot take the place of function. No arrangement of canals and pipes can possibly bring water when there is none. However, if there is water, the arrangement of the piping may hinder its flow. In the same way, form cannot supply what only function can give. The most you can expect of form is that it should not hinder function.

So when we look at the form of New Testament churches, we will also be seeking to understand the way they functioned.

Love and fellowship
In the New Testament it is apparent that the church is a group of people who have entered into a relationship with God through Jesus Christ. Loving God, they also love one another as brothers and sisters. They meet together regularly to worship God, to hear God's word, to teach one another and to join together in remembering Jesus' death by eating bread and drinking wine. Discipline for immoral members may also take place at such a meeting (1 Corinthians 5:4, 5).

Within the membership of the church there should be practical support for one another, encouraging the weak, relieving need, providing for gifts to be exercised. The love displayed to one another should be a potent sign to those who are not members (John 13:35).

The local church
Centralised control is at the root of much of the system of denominations. Churches in most denominations are answerable to their central authority. Because each grouping of churches has a different central authority, the denominations are separate. The ecumenical movement would like to see a single central authority. We must now examine whether this was the situation which existed in the early church. Were the local churches part of a hierarchical interconnected structure with authority coming from a central body, or, if not, to what extent were they autonomous and self-governing?

In Acts 15 we find Paul and Barnabas in Antioch, having returned from their missionary journey among the Gentiles, being challenged by strict Jews who wanted to see the Gentile converts circumcised and taught to keep the law of Moses. It was decided that Paul and Barnabas with some other representatives should go to Jerusalem to ask the apostles (the 'Twelve') and the elders of the Jerusalem church about this matter. The subsequent meeting was what is now known as 'the council of Jerusalem'. Does this passage mean that the leaders in Jerusalem governed other churches such as Antioch? Was there centralised control?

One does not need to suppose such control to justify a matter like this being referred to Jerusalem. The twelve who had been with Jesus throughout his ministry were there. The elders of the Jerusalem church were the longest serving leaders of the first church in existence. The New Testament scriptures were not available for consultation. It is therefore not surprising that such an important matter should be referred to those who knew most about the origins of Christianity.

The subsequent letter to be sent to Gentile churches gives no indication of continuing control. Beyond the moderate advice, the conclusion is (Acts 15:28):

It seemed good to the Holy Spirit and to us not to burden you with anything beyond the following requirements.

Would not centralised control over all churches mean the imposition of further requirements and greater burdens than this?

However, you may consider that certain leaders had control over a number of churches, and so there must have been a hierarchy within the church. We must look at the function of some of those leaders.

Peter and the local churches

Peter confessed Jesus to be the Christ, and was specifically blessed by Christ at that time (Matthew 16:17–19). In particular, Christ said, 'You are Peter, and on this rock I will build my church' (v. 18) and 'I will give you the keys of the kingdom of heaven; whatever you bind on earth will be bound in heaven' (v. 19). Some have seen in these words a declaration that Peter would be the earthly leader of the worldwide church, exercising centralised control. We need to look carefully into this matter, and consider the context of other parts of the New Testament.

Some have suggested that the rock on which the church is built is not Peter but his confession of Jesus as the Christ. However, Ephesians 2:20 describes the church as being 'built on the foundation of the apostles and prophets, with Christ Jesus himself as the chief cornerstone.' The church was built on Peter, but not on Peter alone. It was Peter who delivered the sermon in Acts 2 which was used by God to bring many to salvation, and to build the church in Jerusalem. In one sense, it could be said that in this sermon Peter used the keys of the kingdom of heaven to open the door to those who would respond. However, Jesus promised all his disciples, 'Whatever you bind on earth will be bound in heaven, and whatever you loose on earth will be loosed in heaven' (Matthew 18:18), so Peter's ministry was not unique in this.

In Galatians 2:11–14 we find Peter criticised by Paul for his inconsistency. In Antioch Peter had eaten with the Gentiles, but when certain strict Jews came from the apostle James, Peter separated himself from the Gentiles. This certainly does not give the impression of a leader in overall control of all the churches.

In Galatians 2:7–9 Paul records the outcome of his meeting with the apostles in Jerusalem. It was agreed that Paul should carry the gospel to the Gentiles, and James, Peter and John should take the gospel to the Jews. Verse 7 notes that 'Peter had been given the task of preaching the gospel to the Jews.' Once again, we do not see Peter as the overall leader of all the churches, Jewish and Gentile.

There is no indication to be readily seen in the New Testament that Peter had particular responsibility for a group of churches. What is more, nothing is said to show that Peter's position in the church would be handed on to a successor. If Peter had overall control of all the local churches, and if in this way one man was to exercise centralised control throughout the ages, one would expect the New Testament to give details of how the leadership was to be passed on.

Paul and the local churches
It is obvious that Paul was concerned for a number of churches. When listing the problems he has encountered, he concludes, 'Besides everything else, I face daily the pressure of my concern for all the churches' (2 Corinthians 11:28). His epistles show that besides a pastoral concern for these various churches, he also had an authority to wield over them. He speaks of 'the authority the Lord gave us for building you up rather than pulling you down' (2 Corinthians 10:8). This was not simply an authority over the Corinthian church. He could give commands to the Thessalonians also (2 Thessalonians 3:6–15). He directed Titus to put in order what was defective in the church in Crete and to appoint elders there (Titus 1:5).

Does this indicate centralised control over a group of churches? Not necessarily. It must be remembered that Paul was the one who preached the gospel to these people in the first place, and through whom the churches came into being. He was eager to revisit the churches to see how they were faring (Acts 15:36). When it was obvious that his final visit had been paid, he summoned the elders of Ephesus to a meeting in Miletus, and gave them his parting injunctions (Acts 20:17–38). When he was not able to visit churches, he wrote to them instead.

In fact, Paul was exercising the role of the church planter or missionary. A missionary should be rather like the scaffolding around a building. When the structure is in place and functioning, the scaffolding is to be taken away. We are not given any hint that in the future the ministry which Paul exercised for the churches he had planted was to be carried on by anyone else. It was a temporary task, only necessary until the churches could stand on their own feet.

The alternative interpretation is that there was a group of 'Paul's churches', with Paul as the head. This would mean that there were other groups of churches, with other apostles in charge of them. Could Paul have been happy with such a situation? Hardly so, if you read what he says in 1 Corinthians 1:12 about those who say 'I follow Paul' or 'I follow Apollos' or 'I follow Cephas [Peter]' or 'I follow Christ'.

The evidence seems to point to Paul having temporary pastoral oversight over the churches which he had planted, until such time as these churches could stand on their own feet as independent congregations.

Bishops and the local churches

At the present day, in some denominations, the people who have charge of a number of churches are called bishops. The New Testament certainly speaks about bishops. Are we therefore to conclude that the New Testament envisages people who have control over a number of churches?

There are two terms used in the epistles, 'bishop' and 'elder'. The Greek for 'bishop' is *episkopos* (from which we get words such as 'episcopal'), which means 'an overseer' (*epi* meaning 'upon' or 'over', and *skopos* being at the root of English words for seeing, such as 'microscope' and 'telescope'). The Greek for the word 'elder' is *presbuteros* (from which we get words such as 'presbyterian'), which means 'older one'.

It is clear that 'elder' and 'overseer' refer to the same office. In Titus 1:5 Paul reminds Titus that he left him in Crete to appoint elders, and he continues in v. 7 saying, 'Since an overseer . . .' The two words are synonymous.

The requirements for an elder are listed in 1 Timothy 3:2–7 and in Titus 1:7–9. From these some of his responsibilities can be seen. He needs to take care of the church (1 Timothy 3:5), and perhaps this has an overtone of 'ruling'. He needs to be doctrinally sound so that he may 'encourage others by sound doctrine' and also 'refute those who oppose it' (Titus 1:9). Those who take care of (rule) the church well deserve a 'double honour, especially those whose work is preaching and teaching' (1 Timothy 5:17). It seems most likely that this 'double honour' refers to a full financial remuneration for those elders who work full time for the church. The elders of the church also need to pray for healing for the sick (James 5:14).

It was Paul's custom to appoint elders in every church which was planted (Acts 14:23; Titus 1:5). Whenever elders or overseers are mentioned in the New Testament, they are always in the plural. Elders ('bishops') did not exercise authority over several churches. Rather, each church had a number of elders. They were the joint leaders of the local church, and exercised a spiritual ministry among the members. Peter exhorts the elders to be shepherds of God's flock (1 Peter 5:1–4), showing that the function of the elder is pastoral.

The office of elder is not just an idea of Paul's. Peter and James also speak as if churches will by nature have elders over them. Every church today needs leaders. There is a need for those who will take care of the church, exercise authority, give instruction in sound doctrine, show pastoral care, preach and teach. All the verses mentioned here about elders speak of activities which are still of vital concern. Therefore, whatever we call them, we do still need elders in every church who will perform these functions.

The point for us to note is that in the New Testament bishops did not exercise control over a number of churches (with archbishops over the bishops). Rather, bishops were elders with a pastoral ministry in the local church.

Local but not isolated

The picture so far emerging in this chapter has been weighted towards individual autonomous churches. In the New Testament there was also interchange and fellowship between churches.

For one thing, there were visiting speakers which went from one local church to another. Paul urged Apollos to visit the Corinthians (1 Corinthians 16:12). Paul was sending to Corinth 'the brother who is praised by all the churches for his service to the gospel' (2 Corinthians 8:18), whoever that may have been. Paul longed to visit Rome, a church he had not planted, in order to preach the gospel there and reap a harvest (Romans 1:9–13). John gives warnings about visiting speakers who are adrift in their doctrine: such people are not to be received or even welcomed (2 John 9–11).

There were greetings passed between members of different churches (Romans 16; Colossians 4:14–15) and even between churches (1 Corinthians 16:19–20). Various individuals travelled from one church to another, and were mentioned as those deserving a welcome (Romans 16:1–2; Colossians 4:10). These things indicate the warmth of fellowship which existed between churches and between believers in New Testament times.

The greatest example of concern and fellowship is shown by the way in which Gentile churches came to the aid of churches in Judea when their members were in need. This first came about by prophecy in Antioch (Acts 11:27–30), and was the cause of the most detailed passage on giving within the New Testament, in 2 Corinthians chapters 8 and 9.

We might expect that independent churches would result in endless divisions. In fact, the opposite was true. Because the churches had fellowship and showed love for one another, there was unity between them which was visible to all around.

Gifts and ministries

The church universal is likened to a building, with the apostles and prophets as the foundation and Christ as the chief cornerstone (Ephesians 2:20). The local church is described as supplied with gifts from Christ, apostles, prophets, evangelists and pastor/teachers (Ephesians 4:11). The function of these ministries is so that the church may be built up, and also 'to prepare God's people for works of service' (v. 12). So we can expect the true New Testament church to be supplied with a number of people who have spiritual gifting from God to function in this way.

We have a glimpse of this at the beginning of Acts 13; in the Antioch church there were a number of prophets and teachers, who met together to worship the Lord and fast (v. 2). Perhaps this was a meeting not of the whole church but of some of the leaders, but it shows that there were a number of them and they were characterised by spiritual gifts.

Spiritual gifts are described in 1 Corinthians 12. They are the *charismata*, from which we derive the word 'charismatic'. These are all gifts distributed among the members of the church, 'the manifestation of the Spirit for the common good' (v. 7). It is apparent from 1 Corinthians 14 that the 'common good' which is intended is that 'the church may be edified' (v. 5) when these gifts are exercised in church meetings. If God distributes among his people a multiplicity of gifts and ministries for the good of all and the building up of the church, then it is surely the case that these gifts should be allowed full expression in the church.

1 Corinthians 14:26 comes nearest to showing us what it was like when the early church met together. Paul says, 'When you come together, everyone has a hymn, or a word of instruction, a revelation, a tongue or an interpretation'. We cannot be sure whether Paul is telling them what should happen, or whether he is describing what does happen. Either way, though he lays down principles to regulate such meetings, and stipulates that 'everything should be done in a fitting and orderly way' (v. 40), in no way does he indicate that he rejects meetings taking such a form.

It appears, then, that the form of at least one New Testament church was such that a large number of people (all the believers?) could take part in the meetings.

In the New Testament the priesthood of all believers is evident. Christ has 'made us to be a kingdom and priests to serve his God and Father' (Revelation 1:6). We are 'a kingdom and priests to serve our God' (Revelation 5:10), 'a royal priesthood, a holy nation, a people belonging to God' (1 Peter 2:9).

In the New Testament all members were encouraged to exercise the gifts with which God had endowed them. In fact, we can see how the apostles, prophets, evangelists and pastor/teachers operated 'to prepare God's people for works of service' (Ephesians 4:12). In facilitating the ministries they were developing new apostles, prophets, evangelists and pastor/teachers. The ground was being laid for the multiplication of the church. The church is like a body, with Christ as head, which 'grows and builds itself up in love, as each part does its work' (Ephesians 4:16).

Meeting places

If we were able to attend one of the church meetings in those early days, we would no doubt be impressed by the simplicity of everything.

There were no church buildings. Instead, meetings took place in houses; the church in their/her/your house is the common phrase (Romans 16:5; 1 Corinthians 16:19; Colossians 4:15; Philemon 2).

It is important to point out that these were churches in homes. They were not housegroups (of a central church) or cells (under centralised control). They were churches in their own right.

Acts 20:7-12 gives an interesting insight into the church meeting together. They had a visiting speaker (Paul), they met together to break bread (the Lord's supper), they continued from evening until midnight (perhaps because some of the believers were slaves and could not get away earlier), and they met in the upper room of a house.

It is true that Paul discussed in the lecture hall of Tyrannus (Acts 19:9), but this seems to have been an evangelistic discussion group rather than a church, and took place every day.

Many churches nowadays seem to be based on the model of a lecture, or of a ceremonial rite. A meeting in a home may be more informal, more like a family gathering. It is perhaps not insignificant that in Luke 15, when the prodigal son returns home, he is met with a family party, complete with singing, dancing and joyful celebration. You can do that sort of thing in a home!

Traditions

There is nothing wrong in traditions in themselves. In fact, Paul speaks of Christian traditions (1 Corinthians 11:12, 2 Thessalonians 2:15, 3:6). The traditions against which Jesus spoke are those which run counter to God's commands (Matthew 15:3, Mark 7:8). Let us examine the key aspects of the New Testament church against which we need to measure our own.

The traditions which divide the Christian church into denominations obstruct Jesus' desire for the unity of his people. If these layers could be stripped away so that what remains is true to the New Testament, would not that be a good thing? Aspects of early Christian church life could actually bring a breath of fresh air (or a breath of God's Spirit).

Meeting in a home meant that churches were of necessity limited in size. When you have a small group, everyone knows everyone else. Love, fellowship and encouragement are worked out in practice. You can get to know each member and their needs, and can pray for each other and bear one another's burdens.

In a small group you cannot shirk your responsibilities and hide behind other people. God dispersed his gifts among the members of the church, and each one was encouraged to play his or her part and to grow in the gifts which God has given. You could not necessarily leave the work of evangelism to a minister or missionary. Because there were not many members, the contribution of each one was vital. Each church was autonomous, so although encouragement, teaching and advice were available from mature visiting believers, the church was responsible for its own life and conduct, looking to God for his direction and help.

Because all the members were involved and accepted responsibility, the message was spread to unbelievers rapidly. The overheads in planting a new church were few. This contrasts with many Christian groups today, when planting a new church may involve great expense in training up a minister and erecting a building. Starting a new church in a home costs very little in terms of finance. Involving all the members and developing their gifts meant that leaders for these new churches were constantly being multiplied. It appears that not only was there an increase in the number of people who believed, the churches themselves 'grew daily in numbers' (Acts 16:5). These were churches which planted churches which planted churches.

Just as we tend to judge a church primarily by its form, so we tend to cling on to the forms which we know and love. We need to evaluate how our churches function in the light of how New Testament churches functioned. Above all, we need to see clearly through the fog of our traditions to discern what the scriptures indicate are the most important aspects of church life. How does your church compare with those in New Testament times?

Postscript

In this book I have sought to demonstrate principles for handling the scriptures which lead to good and right interpretations. I have attempted to show how applying these principles brings out the main themes of the Bible. I have tried to chop down some of the weeds which have obscured these main themes.

Now it is for you to say whether I have succeeded in these aims. At the end of Chapter 2 I suggested a list of principles for considering a particular teaching or theme. These were the following:

1 *Start with what is clear.*
2 *Examine the context of the rest of the Bible.*
3 *Consider the context of the world around us.*
4 *Examine how broad the foundation is.*
5 *Be prepared to admit your ignorance.*
6 *How much does it matter?*

I have tried to keep to these principles when considering Biblical themes throughout this book. In particular, the following themes showed themselves as being sewed through and through the Bible:

    a Christ is the *major theme* of all the scriptures.
    b Christ offered *one sacrifice* for sin, once for all.
    c There is *one way of salvation* through Christ.
    d There is *one people of God*, the church of Christ, Jew and Gentile.
    e We are now *not under the Law, but under grace*.

If you disagreed with my conclusions in particular chapters, then you need to consider whether I have strayed from my principles, or else whether these principles are not right, or whether the list of principles is incomplete.

Some would say that the list certainly is incomplete. There are three other possibilities which keep pushing themselves forward as principles. We have encountered them in many places within this book, and have rejected them. It is only right that now they should be unmasked and recognised as the impostors which they are.

A 'Interpret as literally as you can'

We saw in Chapter 2 that it is impossible to interpret all of the Bible literally. If you try to do so, you make the Bible tear itself apart. The difficult task is knowing which parts to interpret literally and which figuratively. Where did you get the idea that you should interpret it as literally as possible? Does the Bible teach this? Certainly Christ did not (see John 6:63 for instance). The New Testament regularly gives spiritual interpretations for that which was literal and physical in the Old. If we seek an interpretation which is as literal as possible, then we not only force a conflict between the Bible and the real world, we provoke conflict between different parts of the Bible. This false principle has the appearance of giving supreme honour to the scriptures, but instead it brings dishonour on them.

B 'Give major emphasis to the Old Testament'

The Old Testament is the inspired word of God, just as the New is. However, we have been given a good pair of spectacles with which to read the Old: read it with the vision which the New Testament gives. When the Old Testament speaks of literal temple, priests, continual sacrifices, then the New Testament shows us the spiritual reality which these things represent. In particular, the Law is the governing factor in the Old Testament; now it no longer holds sway over us, but is replaced by grace.

C 'Let your traditions be supreme'

The traditions of your own church are no doubt precious to you. However, we should not allow them to distort what the Bible is saying. Jesus accused some of nullifying the word of God for the sake of their tradition (Matthew 15:6). This also goes for the traditional teaching you have heard. You may have a great love and respect for the leaders from whom you have heard these things. But they are only human, after all, and they may be wrong. Be prepared to investigate their teachings in the light of the Bible and see whether their interpretations are wisely based.

As I said, you may have disagreed with the conclusions I reached in some of the chapters in this book. If you did, then consider that the disagreement may be because you have been giving ear to one or other of these three impostors. I beg you to consider whether these things are snagging your interpretation. It is vital for you to approach the scriptures aright because they 'are written that you may believe that Jesus is the Christ, the Son of God, and that by believing you may have life through his name' (John 20:31). Freeing yourself from these false principles may help you to get things straight—from the Bible.

www.ingramcontent.com/pod-product-compliance
Lightning Source LLC
Chambersburg PA
CBHW052057070526
44584CB00017B/2224